From Ghetto to Augusta

An Uplifting Golf Story of Triumph over Tragedy

By Michael Kelm

Preface

Jack Jeffers is a rebellious teenager who was abandoned at birth. He lived on the streets of Atlanta's toughest neighborhoods. By age 16, he had bounced around through a dozen different foster families. He spent time in juvie, slung drugs, and nearly beat his foster parent to death. With his life spiraling downward following another foray with the law, he is rescued by an unlikely hero.

Glenn Andrews was an old-school Southern lawyer. He was crusty, sage, and no nonesense. His life has been in shambles following the tragic death of his wife and son. In a sheer act of desperation, he looks to the foster system as a last-ditch attempt to fill the massive void in his life.

Glenn quickly realizes that he and Jack are a difficult match. Jack wants no part of authority, school, work, or the structure living under Glenn's roof requires. Their tug-of-war turns into a dust-up with one of Jack's street friends. Facing a possible return back to the ghetto, Jack is forced to take a job at Glenn's country club as a caddie. He loathes aristocrats, Southern gentlemen, and everything associated with country club opulence. Yet, Jack ultimately overcomes much of his class bias to become among the Club's most outstanding caddies. As part of the job, he gets exposed to the riggers of work and responsibility as well as well-mannered, educated people. He also gets exposed to the game of golf.

Jack as a caddie has no inclination to play golf. But one day, he spots the most attractive girl alive on the course playing with several boys their age. He quickly realizes that his only chance with this girl is to clean up his act and become a golfer.

The motivation of a girl takes him in an exciting direction. After one lesson and just an hour on the range, he realizes golf comes very naturally to him. His golf instructor calls him a generational phenomenon. He quickly becomes among the best junior golfers at the Club, with a silky swing most golfers would die for. As hoped, his golf game brings him closer to Jen and gives him a newfound purpose- maybe even a new lease on life.

Jack's golf game ascends him to the highest echelons of the sport. Yet he still yearns to understand his roots and the reasons behind his parents' abandonment. That search takes him and Jen on a journey to Scotland, where they find love at the birthplace of golf and an astonishing discovery about Jack's ancestry.

This is the story of a grieving father and a troubled youth who, with the power of golf, forge a lasting bond. Excising the demons of their pasts fosters mutual healing through an extraordinary journey of fame and self-discovery.

In this narrative, we learn how there are many avenues for success…in both golf and life. Using this vivid metaphor, we come to appreciate how playing from an easy, unobstructed fairway does not guarantee success anymore than playing from a difficult hazard guarantees failure. It is how we play the shots we face that ultimately defines us. That is why we play the game.

That is the theme behind "From Ghetto to Augusta".

Dedicated to my Granddaughter,

Riley Merritt Duncan
1/26/2022 - 6/13/2023

Table of Contents

Chapter 1 - Jack learns a new word, Miscreant

Chapter 2 - Jack the Looper

Chapter 3 - Golf, maybe something I am good at

Chapter 4 - Jack takes his game to high school

Chapter 5 - Mending

Chapter 6 - College and the Search for Family

Chapter 7 - Jack Proves Game in Amateur Tournaments

Chapter 8 - Jen's New Boyfriend

Chapter 9 - Off to Scottland

Chapter 10- Jack Finds his Parents

Chapter 11- Pressure Builds as US Amateur looms

Chapter 12- The Masters

Chapter 13- Glenn faces legal Amaggeddon

Chapter 14- An Astonishing Discovery

Copyright 2023
All Right Reserved

Disclaimer:

This is a work of fiction. Unless otherwise indicated, all the names, characters, businesses, places, events and incidents in this book are either the product of the author's imagination or used in a fictitious manner. Any resemblance to actual persons, living or dead, or actual events is purely coincidental.

Chapter 1

Jack learns a new word, Miscreant

I was sitting handcuffed at the police station, talking with the arresting officer. It was about 3 am, and I had just been taken in as an accessory to a car theft. "My name is Jack Jeffers," I told the officer. "I am 16 and live in Jones Creek." The officer said, "You were arrested for stealing a car. Do you want to tell me your side of the story?" I told him my boy Rory picked me up by my place. I had no idea the car was hot. The officer then asked me kind of an obvious question, "Does this friend Rory commonly pick you up in a brand new Mercedes-Benz?" I smiled with a somewhat sheepish grin, knowing I didn't have much of an answer for that.

The officer was motioned out of the interrogation room by another officer. He told me to "wait here" as he exited the room. I remained seated for what seemed like an eternity. As I waited, I could not help but let my mind wander and absorb the unsavory state of this place. The walls bore unsightly stains of uncertain origin, with patches of bare plaster marking spots where hotheads kicked the shit out of the wall. There was also a vile stench reminiscent of downtown alleys where people frequently piss wherever. Even though I was not unfamiliar with this place, my imagination couldn't help but conjure up thoughts of seedy dudes who had once occupied the same chair I was sitting in.

The officer returned a few minutes later and told me that Rory took full responsibility for the theft and said I wasn't involved. "You're cleared," he said. He then told me that I was being released to Glenn Andrews, my foster parent, who was called to pick me up. My first reaction was, "Oh Shit, I am fucked!" Glenn will be pissed.

I sat in the police office for about an hour before Glenn arrived, giving me a little more time to reflect. During that time, I remembered just how much I hated this place. Unfortunately, trouble and police station are like twin sisters. They are hard to separate.

I had been busted a couple of times for theft. I got caught selling pot to kids. I was present in a house that was stormed by a swat team making a drug bust. Then, there was a time I struck a police officer who was trying to arrest me. That cost me a week in juvie. My last incident was when I took a 2x4 to my former foster parent, that nearly killed him. He was beating his wife and deserved to be taken out. That was another 30 days in juvie.

Part of me wants to brush most of this off as just being an abandoned kid who was a victim of circumstance or just being in the wrong place at the wrong time. The other part says Jack, you are a fuck-up whose friends are losers. I know what Glenn is going to say. He'll say, "Jack, I gave you a chance, and you fucked up. You're out!". At some level, I would not blame him for doing that.

When Glenn arrived, he didn't say a word. He didn't have to. The look in his eyes told me all I needed to know. I have been staying with Glenn for a couple of months now. Unfortunately, this is not the first time Glenn has hauled me out of a police station. He drove me back to his house in Jones Creek without uttering a word. His silence was deafening, as they say.

Glenn could be very reflective. He would get these looks where his mind seemed like he was a thousand miles away. Glenn could also be a proverbial hardass. But overall, he wasn't a bad guy once you got beyond the tough exterior. As much as Glenn frustrates the hell out of me at times, I feel lucky he has not kicked my ass out…yet.

Glenn was what they called an old-school Southern lawyer. From what I could gather, he came from a long line of lawyers who worked in the same firm for a hundred years or better. Glenn was like the 5th generation lawyer. I don't know much about the legal profession, but it seems to provide him a pretty nice living. Still, Glenn was no nonsense and strict. He was a hardass, but also a gentleman. Probably a good combination for a successful lawyer I am guessing.

His place is extremely nice and clean, and he always has good food. That is a hundred times better than what I've experienced in Shitsville, as I like to call Southwest Atlanta. Here, I am not beefin' with druggies or dodging bullets. In reality, I am not nearly as bad as many kids. Mostly, I hung out on the streets and tried to escape what was sometimes a living hell at home. I think that was the line they fed to Glenn. Jack was a good kid who just got caught up in bad situations.

Part of me wants to get to know Glenn better. However, every ounce of my programming says Glenn can't be trusted. Every other male in my life has been either a crook or a total shithead. Why should I expect something different this time? That is why I still hang out with my homies, smoking dope or getting drunk. The homies are family. The only family I have ever known. I trust them.

My main man Rory reminds me. Even though I get to ride in this Caddilac and hang out in an upscale suburb, I still the same loser from the hood inside. He's right. I am a 16-year-old without a fucking pot to pee in. I am an orphan–or abandoned kid–who has lived and survived through the dregs of the foster system. I have lived with creeps. I have lived with abusers. Most did not give a shit about me or what I did. Now for the first time, I've got a foster parent who gives a shit. I got lucky, but for how long.

Rory says to "Ride the wave, Dude." Although, every ounce of my wiring says don't get too comfortable. Your ride won't last long.

I am a lot different than guys like Rory. While some may disagree, I have a conscience. That is, I care about people and how they feel. To that end, I must give Glenn his do. He says he took me in because he saw something in me that others didn't. He thought I was smart and had a heart. I don't know about any of that. But I am grateful he brought me into his life when logic suggests no one would want to deal with my shit. I'll give him that.

We arrived back at the house after 45 minutes of stone-cold silence on the road. By this time, it was just starting to get light. While we walked up the stairs, Glenn finally spoke in his typical direct voice. He said, "Get some sleep. We've got church at 11".

I immediately ran upstairs to my bedroom and dove into bed. After what seemed like only a couple of winks, it was Glenn, again, barking and telling me to get my butt out of bed and ready for church. The Church service was agonizingly long this time. I have never been a church-goer–or believer–for that matter. For the few times I have been there, I tune out the holy roller BS. But, admittedly, today's sermon was like a saving grace. The preacher spoke out about extending the hand of mercy to those who falter. That message could not have come at a more critical time. I hope Glenn was listening.

Glenn put his arm around my shoulder on the walk out of church. I don't know what that meant, but it probably meant something. Glenn's emotions rarely extend beyond his rough exterior. He just doesn't exude emotion. He has a purpose behind it this time. I will call it a good sign.

We crossed the street where Glenn's car was parked. Just then, a new Ferrari convertible sped by. Driving the car was some well-dressed dude with his arm around what I would call a trophy babe. Glenn, who was nearly hit by the guy, said something under his breath, probably a 4-letter explicative. He would never express anger in an aggressive manner. Instead, he then looked over at me, almost begging for a reaction. Feeling obligated to speak, I said something that was probably inappropriate, "I hope I am rich like that one day." Glenn's demeanor instantly changes to this stern look of disapproval. I assume he is mad because I gave legitimacy to this asshole driver. Glenn stops before getting into the car and says, "The first step to becoming wealthy is to understand what is valuable. "

Most of Glenn's feeble attempts at philosophy go in one ear and out the other. But for some reason, this one made me think. I was going to ask him what he meant but thought better of it. Glenn reminds me often of Mark Twain's saying that it is better to keep quiet and let people suspect you are ignorant than to speak out and remove all doubt. Sometimes, I have to chuckle at Glenn's dry humor.

Usually, after church, we will go to breakfast at one of the local spots or go over to a friend's house. Today, however, we drove out to the Country Club and had a nice brunch on the patio overlooking the golf course's first hole.

The Club was extremely high-brow, probably even stuffy by most accounts. Back in Shitsville, it would be known as 'rich bitch'. Everyone was dressed well in expensive clothes they probably bought at Neiman Marcus or someplace like that. The place just reeked of old Southern money and affluence. Only prominent people belonged here. I certainly did not belong. But this was Glenn's scene. People knew him. They seemed to like him. He shook a lot of hands.

Most of this shallow socializing just made me cringe. I had to meet people and nod with a smile. Glenn knew I was totally out of my element, too. However, I did like the smell of the freshly cut grass. If you wanted to watch people, this was a good spot. People looked relaxed and seemed to be enjoying themselves. They also seemed to be angling for influence and social prominence. That behavior was fascinating, but cringy. Where I come from, that behavior can get you whacked. It's the norm here.

After we ate, Glenn walked me around, showing me the various amenities at the Club. He took me to where his great-grandfather Andrews was named on a plaque. From what I could gather, great-grandfather Andrews was one of the founding members back in 1910. As we walked, I could not help but see he was trying to communicate something to me, but what? We spent at least an hour watching golfers hit balls by the range. I had never watched golf live before, but I was fascinated by how far a golf ball could travel after being struck by a simple club.

The driving range showed you all shapes and sizes out there. Some golfers were athletic. Some were not. Some that looked athletic swung awkwardly, and the ball would dribble out a short way. Others, who were fat and unathletic, could swing fluidly and hit the ball a mile. I never saw this as something I might want to try, let alone be good at. The notion of me engaging in activities rich people do, barely registered in my consciousness.

Our next stop was the Club locker room. This was unlike anything I had ever seen. At school, lockers were beat-up and smelled like a sweaty jock. This room was beautiful. There was mahogany wood everywhere. It smelled like one of those high-class soap shops. We then walked over to this bulletin board on the wall, and it became apparent what Glenn wanted me to see.

There was a sign that said, "Caddies. Sign Up for the summer. Attend Caddie school on April 5th." Glenn asked me if I knew what a caddie was. I told him, "Yep," I had watched the movie "The Legend of Bagger Vance" and the "Gentlemen's Game." Glenn said, "I would like you to do this."

I said, "No fucking way," in a demonstrative tone such that others in the locker room probably heard."

I thought to myself, this is not my scene at all. I do not even like this place. The last thing I wanted to do was schmooze old fatcats and hustle for tips. I was not going to pimp dudes carrying clubs. I would rather be pimping whores on the streets, to be honest.

Glenn did not respond to my brief tirade but looked at me with that stare I had seen before. I am guessing that we were not done with the topic.

A couple of days passed, and the matter of being a caddie had not come up, fortunately. I wondered if Glenn had forgotten or, better yet, would let this one skate by for good.

Glenn was watching TV, sipping on a Scotch while I was playing a game on my phone. Glenn then asked me something pretty random. "Do you have any homework?" I responded without really thinking through my word choice very carefully. I said "I had a couple of assignments to work through but needed the teacher's help. "So no."
Glenn then threw me an unexpected curveball. "Let me help you," he said.

He approached the table where I pulled out my most challenging math problems, thinking that would set him back on his heels. Glenn then said, "I love this stuff. Let's work through a few of these." I thought, oh great. After about an hour of solving excruciating math problems, I hoped Glenn would get the idea that my head was not in this. With every inch of my being, I needed Glenn to sense my indifference

and angst. Please, Glenn, go back to your movie. Enjoy another Scotch, I thought. But nope!
Glenn then sees my American History book on the table and says, "I know a little about history. What are you studying there?". I told him we were studying post-Civil War reconstruction, thinking the fancy subject title might shut him up for good. Another nope.

He goes on to explain that his Andrews family were originally northerners. In fact, one of his ancestors had died fighting for the Union Army. During Reconstruction, the Andrews moved to Atlanta to defend black families against persecution.

Glenn yammered on about a bunch of stuff I needed help understanding. But I gathered this much. During Reconstruction, there were a lot of northerners who moved to the South to exploit those who were down and out. They called them carpetbaggers. It sounds like Glenn's people moved there to help people. Hmmm.

It was getting close to midnight, and Glenn had thankfully dozed off in his chair as he commonly does. He held his Scotch in his left hand and almost spilled it on himself. I ran over and grabbed it. I then took a sip to finish off the glass.

At about the same time, I heard a quiet knock on the outside window. I went to see who it was. It was Rory and this young girl who probably wasn't a day over 14. I am guessing they had just hooked up in the backseat of his car. He asked me if I was ready to head out. I said, "Sorry, dude, I can't do it tonight." Rory said, "No problem. Hey, can I grab a beer and maybe a quick dip in the pool?" I told him, OK, but you gotta keep it quiet, though, and then get the hell outta here.

Rory and the girl had just undressed and gotten in the pool when I heard this old beat-up truck with a loud muffler out in front. The motor stopped, and a big, burly guy walked up to the door and knocked loudly. I start walking toward the door, and the banging repeats, except it is much louder this time. I crack the door, and the burly 40-ish guy in overalls busts through the door, sending me halfway across the room.

"Where the hell is Darcy!" he shouted in a frantic, almost psychotic tone. He sees activity out back and marches in that direction, knocking over a lamp. With all the commotion, Glenn gets out of his chair and confronts this guy. "I know you've got Darcy. I tracked her from her cell phone. Where the fuck is she?" this guy barks out. Glenn says, "I have no idea what you are talking about." The burly guy, who must be an angry father, sees Darcy getting out of the pool stark naked. "Oh shit," I thought to myself. The guy shouts out with an enraged expression on his face, "There she is, you piece of shit," assuming Glenn was a participant in his daughter's apparent loss of virtue. He then throws Glenn through the sliding glass window and runs outside to grab his daughter. They both leave in one of those heated father-child skirmishes you see in the movies.

Glenn was lying still face down on the outside patio floor with cuts on his arm. A couple looked pretty deep, with a lot of blood draining out. He finally rolls over and gathers himself, showing bruises and some minor scratches on his face. Fortunately, he seems OK. I hand him a towel that he wraps around his arm. I motioned to Rory that he needed to get the hell out of there. I went over to assist Glenn back inside. Rory finally leaves after first stopping by the fridge to grab a beer or two for the road.

Glenn sits for a minute before becoming more lucid. He instructed me to grab the keys and drive him to the emergency room. I still needed my license, but I passed my learners a while back. For this kid, any driving trip is exciting. "Let's go," I said.

I may have spoken a little early about enjoying a trip behind the wheel. Glenn's had this look of disgust on his face. Glenn may have been silent, but you could tell he was seething inside. His silence was deafening, as they say. He wouldn't even talk when I needed directions to the hospital. He would just point.

We arrived in the emergency room, and Glenn signed into the hospital registry. He then approached where I sat in the waiting room and spoke. In the few months I have lived at Glenn's, he has been generally quiet and reflective. He was a man of view words, but when he said something to say, it was generally something he was serious about. Glenn said, looking me directly in the eyes, "I want you to sit here and not move. Look at everyone who walks in this door and reflect upon their lives and the circumstances that may have brought them here." He paused, then said, "Jack, you're a smart kid. Do you want to spend your life going between the police station and the emergency room?. Think about it. I want to believe you're better than this."

Glenn then strode out of the waiting room into the treatment area. I had initially considered joking about needing to piss but thought the better of it. As Glenn had ordered, I sat there, watching and reflecting.

I stayed in that chair for what seemed like forever. During that time, I saw a couple of teenagers who were in a horrific crash, a dude who had been knifed along with a couple of others with what seemed like drug overdoses. One was even a teenage girl who was pronounced dead at the scene.

Glenn thinks this stuff is going to freak me out. Hey Glenn, I have news for you; I have seen much worse shit in my day. Probably more than Glenn realizes. When you are a product of the foster system from Shitsville, Georgia, you are no stranger to guns, drugs, violence, and blood.

Glenn eventually came out with his arm heavily wrapped. He had a few bandaids on his face and a big bandage around his head. I am assuming that meant he had a concussion.

I pulled the car around to the door, where an orderly helped Glenn get into the car. From there, we drove over to Dan's Diner for breakfast and sat in the corner to avoid attention. By this time, the sun was rising, and Glenn was moving slowly but seemed to gain some energy. We made one last stop at the Home Depot to pick up a sheet of plywood to cover the broken window on the patio.

Once home, I helped Glenn out of the car and climbed into bed. He was visibly sore and cut up, but thankfully OK. I went to my room and lay in bed, wondering what was in store for me and what I would do if Glenn sent me back into the system.

Glenn slept until nearly 8 pm. I even checked on him several times to ensure he hadn't croaked. The last time I came in, Glenn was sitting in bed reading some texts. I asked him if he wanted anything to eat. He said, "Thanks. That would be great". I am no cook, but I threw a few leftovers into the microwave. He seemed appreciative.

By the time I got up the next morning, It was a sunny spring day, and Glenn had already been up. He put on a pot of coffee and was making breakfast. As he poured me a cup of coffee, he said, "Thanks for cleaning up the glass and putting up the plywood." I said, "Sure', but was thinking with relief, could his remark be a sign that the ax may not be falling after all?

He put a plate of scrambled eggs and grits in front of me and said, "Let's talk about the other night." Glenn said, "Jack, I gathered that your friend was, let's say, misbehaving with an underage girl, and the two of them showed up on our doorstep. You let them in our house to partake in the pool and the girl's father discovered their whereabouts. He came here extremely angry to rescue his daughter. Do I have this right so far?" I said, "Yes, sir, I think you've got it accurately."

Glenn said, "I figured I had incurred approximately $1500 in damages. And that does not account for the emergency room visit or my pain and suffering, which I will not be pursuing. Who should pay me restitution?" I said "Restitution"? He countered and said, "Compensation for my injury and loss." I thought about it briefly and then said, "The big burly dude. He caused the damage." I said. Glen then came back and said, "No. This is your fault for allowing miscreants onto our property. As the judge and jury here, I find you guilty and order you to pay me $1500 in restitution".

I fired back at Glenn with a more heated response. "Why am I responsible for the shit caused by other people?" Glenn said, "I could give you a lengthy legal justification supported by case law and precedent, but let me dumb it down. Here is an old axiom. You are judged by the company you keep. Hang out with fuck-ups, you'll eventually get fucked up. It is as simple as that."

I wanted to counter Glenn with some clever come-back, but Glenn as I have learned, is skilled at arguing a case. And he was right. I realized after some reflecting, I was in a lot of trouble because I was hanging with losers and troublemakers...or what Glenn so kindly referred to as 'miscreants.'

Glenn then pulled out this contract he and I signed when I came to live here. These were the 'house rules,' as he called them, that I had to follow while here. They were all a part of what Glen called 'our gentleman's arrangement .' They stated I must:
- Stay out of trouble
- Stay in school
- Work to earn my own money
- Be respectful, and don't steal from me
- Go to church

He instructed me when I first came here that I either follow these or else I'll send you back. I did not get the feeling Glenn was one of those 'zero-tolerance' types. Still, he has undergone what appears to be a change from tolerance to very seriousness. I need to take heed,

Glenn sternly said, "Jack, I consider that you have violated our agreement on three counts." As he spoke, he wrote the three on a piece of paper. The three counts included were:
1) You did not stay out of trouble
2) You have not worked to earn money
3) You owe me $1500

In a rare moment of emotional exposure, Glen said, "Jack, I do like you and care about you. If I hadn't, we would have been gone after your last visit to the police station. At the same time, I can't live my life wondering if you are out in the middle of the AM getting into trouble, or if I am going to get a call from the police, or if some big burly dude is going to come in here and throw me through a sliding-glass window.

I want to hear your proposal for remedying these breaches in our agreement. And there is also the matter of damages. If I am satisfied with your proposal, we will amend the contract forthwith. If I reject your proposal, we are done. You, therefore, need to think about your response carefully. Spend today giving this careful thought, and return for your official response for my consideration at noon tomorrow. OK?" I nodded and went up to my room.

I laid in bed, scared shitless, wondering what I was going to do. Part of me was angry and wanted to tell Glenn to stick it where the sun doesn't shine. At the same time, once I put my emotions aside, I realize I've got a lot of reasons to stay. My entire life is teetering in the balance right now, and I could fall either direction based on my actions. What am I going to do????

I spent most of that day and night just hanging out in my room, listening to music and reflecting upon my dilemma. The following day, I returned to the kitchen one minute before noon with a plan. I pray to God that Glenn finds it acceptable. Even though part of me doesn't give a shit, I really want to stay.

Glenn sat down across from me and seemed anxious to get on with it. "Tell me what you have come up with," he said. I told him, feeling somewhat sheepish, "

1) I will no longer sneak out at night.
   2) I will stop all communication with old friends from Shitsville, and
   3) I will caddie at the Club to pay you the money I owe.

As I spoke, Glenn wrote these one at a time onto the bottom of our previous agreement under the heading he called Amendment. He instructed me to Sign it, which I did. He followed up, signed it, and said, "Good. I accept your proposal. We are done here."
He then got up as quickly as he sat down. In a very matter-of-fact way, he returned to his chair and grabbed his reading glasses and book. That was Glenn.

Chapter 2

Jack the Looper

This afternoon, I am headed to my first Caddie lesson. Going to Caddie school was an essential part of the renegotiation with Glenn. While I may have been adamantly against it initially, maybe even hostile, I agreed to see it out with a good attitude. Glenn says a sign of strength and integrity is to 'stand by your decisions.' And, once you make a commitment, 'always do what you say you are going to do,' especially when people are counting on you. So here we go.

Caddie School - Day 1

Overall, the first lesson was alright, certainly better than I expected. The Instructor was in his early 20s and had been 'looping' as it is called, for about three years, mainly at Eastgate, which was a pretty exclusive course on the Eastside. He was cool and not arrogant or anything like that. He said he spends more time traveling as a caddie instructor than looping on the course.

The first lesson was a very simple axiom. The instructor said 90% of your success in life can be attributed to following this simple axiom. "Show Up. Keep Up. and Shut Up". That is, golfers expect you to be there when they start. A late loop is a dead loop, he explained. Secondly, you have to stay with your group. You can only do your job if you are caught up and engaged with your golfer. Finally, golf is a game of concentration. Golfers do not want to hear extraneous conversations. Only speak if asked or it is required to help the golfer. Never talk when another player is hitting.

I explained this to Glenn on the drive home. Funny, I think he sees himself as an armchair philosopher and likes quips and quotes. I was right. "Show Up. Keep Up. and Shut Up. I like that," Glenn said.

Caddie School - Day 2

On Day 2, we learned about Rules and Etiquette. My first reaction was that there are a shitload of rules. The Instructor handed us all this little book and said, "Read it, know it, use it." I asked him if all golfers have to know all this stuff, and he said, "They do." He then got into the part about how golfers are self-policing. That is, golf is the only game where players call penalties on themselves. Then, I asked what I thought was an intelligent question. "If a player doesn't know a rule, then ignorance is bliss, right?". The Instructor said, not quite. He explained that one of the game's most embarrassing and dishonorable aspects is when an opponent calls you out for not imposing a penalty on yourself. Wow. I thought.

We spent the next hour reading this little book where the guys–and one girl–would ask questions. Most of this stuff blew right over my head. Having never been on the course, little of this made sense. I explained this to Glenn, who said, "Jack, we have some daylight left; why don't we play a few holes."

Glenn grabbed a golf cart and threw his clubs in the back, and he played a few holes as I watched. I liked driving the cart. Glenn told me I was technically not allowed to play as a member, so I didn't even ask. I just watched. Glenn seems pretty good. He will not be confused with Michael Jordan but is not a wimp, either. His swing appears fluid and effortless. He says fluid and effortless are what you want—never herky-jerky.

He went on to explain the various tees, the black tees, the blues, white, and red, and how different people, depending on their skill level, hit from other places. There was also this thing called handicap, which I didn't really get, that adjusts your score so that a lousy player can compete against a strong player. He talked about replacing divots and ball marks on the green and techniques for both. He gave me a couple to practice on.

I think Glenn really enjoyed the camaraderie. Golf was obviously important to him, and I think it brought him joy to share his world with someone else. Also, I got the impression, for the first time, that Glenn was trying to sell me. He could build my interest by showing me this stuff and creating something we could share. I don't know..

The day ended with us sitting up on the deck of the golf lounge and having something to eat. I looked around and observed some of the exchanges. Guys were talking about their game. There was a bad shot there or a missed putt over there. Golf created a reason for guys to hang out. I did not sense attitudes or arrogance, just regular brah interaction.

A couple of guys came over to say hi to Glenn. He introduced me as a new caddie who would join the team shortly, as if he were trying to sell my services. I thanked Glenn for doing that. He made me feel like I mattered.

.

Caddie School - Day 3

Day 3 was about Analysis and Insight. I was puzzled initially, but it finally made sense. Some golfers just want their bags carried. Other golfers wish to rely upon a caddie's experience and knowledge of the course. The hope is that a caddie gains unique insight over time that will help the player score better. The Instructor said, "Caddies on the Pro Tour earn 6-digit incomes by being skillful at analysis and insight." My first reaction was that I doubt I could offer much in that regard. My insight will comprise, 'hit it that way,' as
I pointed in some direction. I chuckled to myself.

The Instructor explained that when you are on the course, you should think of yourself as a sponge that watches and absorbs everything around you. Where are the best places to hit the ball to avoid trouble? Where are the obstacles that may affect a shot, like hanging tree limbs or deep rough, especially those not in view? Where are the holes on the green, and where should the ball land to best get there? The answers to these are all influenced by whether the player is a lowball, highball, or not a straight-ball hitter. Then, you have the speed and the contour of the greens. "It all matters," he said. "These are things you will learn if you train your mind to watch and observe."

We spent the next hour or so in the loop shed, talking amongst ourselves. Tim Riley, one of the trainees, and I were conversing, and he said, "Did you know that Bobby Jones used to play here all the time?". I then asked him with a puzzled expression, "Who is Bobby Jones?" He said, "OMG," and proceeded to tell me about this guy who is obviously famous in the golfing world.

He explains how Bobby Jones was the greatest golfer ever to play the game. He was from Georgia and lived back in the 1900s. Jones had this incredibly smooth golf swing that came to him almost naturally. Even though he was famous for winning major tournaments, he was best known for being a gentleman in the sport. Jones won 13 major championships, including the US and British Open. He is the only golfer to have won all four major tournaments in a single year, a feat known as the Grand Slam. Jones designed and was a founder of Augusta National Golf Club. That is where they play the Masters. He also said that Bobby never played for money but remained an amateur and retired from competitive golf in his prime of life.

Most of the facts he threw out did not make sense to me. I kept nodding as he spoke and threw out an occasional 'wow' or two to sound amazed. I did not want Tim to think I was a total dipshit or something.

On the way home, I asked Glenn if he had heard of Bobby Jones. Boy, that set Glenn into motion. The normally quiet, man-of-a-few-words turned into a firehose of facts. I could hardly keep up, but it did allow me to understand golf and its history in greater detail. Terms like The Masters, Major tournaments, and Amateur vs Profession were totally foreign. Still, I had an encyclopedia sitting right next to me.

Glenn told me a couple of interesting things about Bobby Jones. Jones was a lawyer, and his Grandfather Andrews periodically worked with Bobby on cases. They would play together at the Club whenever Bobby was in town. Grandfather Andrews would also join Bobby whenever they could over at the East Lake Golf Course south of here, Bobby's home course.

Glenn also mentioned that while Bobby was born into an aristocratic family, Jones was a staunch supporter of the under-served class. He frequently donated his time and wealth to help the disadvantaged whenever possible. Grandfather Andrews and Jones shared that viewpoint.

Sitting in the car listening, I could not help but think this Bobby Jones guy was an OK dude. When I hear terms like 'aristocrat' or 'southern gentlemen,' admittedly, I conjure up many negative connotations. Glenn says, "The reality is that poor people are rarely able to help others. While it may be fashionable to disdain the wealthy, at least they are in a position to help people in meaningful ways." That made sense, and I nodded. As I reflected on the stories about Jones, it occurred to me that perhaps there are rich people who do good by people using their power and influence. Jones sounds like one of the good guys.

Caddie School - Day 4

Day 4 was a day to get out on the course and practice some of the principles the Instructor had discussed. A 4-some from the Club volunteered to play and let our class carry bags, assist golfers with club selection, and help with other tasks such as replacing divots, lining up putts, and such.

I got called out several times for making stupid errors, like walking on another putter's line and talking when other players were hitting—stuff like that. Almost everyone did something wrong at some point. It is incredible how being a good caddie boils down to a lot of little details.

One of my biggest takeaways was that you need to be watching all the golfers, not just your golfer. Often, it is easy to get in the way of other golfers not realizing it. You must keep your head on a swivel and observe everything around you.

During the practice round, when it wasn't your turn to caddie, you had time to look, take in the course, and observe things happening on adjoining holes. Standing on the cart path during one of those moments, I noticed this beautiful young redheaded golfer playing on the hole next to me. She seemed short but confident, almost like she was leading her male playing partners around. She was about my age, judging more by the guys she was playing with than by looking at her.

Most of the players at the Club are older, primarily seniors. Some younger families are at the Club, but you don't see many. I asked Glenn about that, and he said it was expensive to play here. He says the Club likes younger members, but few can afford it.

After returning to the loop shed, I asked a couple of established loopers if they knew who that beautiful red-haired girl was. One of the guys had looped for her family. Her name was Jen Laird. She is 'very fine,' he said, speaking in a sly, sultry tone. She lives with her grandmother, who has been a member of the Club forever. "She does not seem to have trouble attracting male company," he said. He then added, "I get a real kick out of some of those old farts who think they have enough game or wallet to get close to her. It is almost embarrassing to watch at times."

I asked Glenn if he knew anyone at the Club named Laird. He said, "Sure. Isla Laird has been a member for a long time. She was married to James, but he died about five years ago. He played golf with James a few times. I remember him being a true gentleman. Did not know Isla."

I explained my interest in the girl who played out there. He just smiled.

Caddie School - Day 5

Today was the second of the 2-day hands-on instruction. Each of us would be paired up with a Club member who would observe our work and offer advice. At the end of the round, they would submit a report to the Caddie committee. Those who did well during this evaluation would enter the loop pool with a senior. The senior would accompany the junior looper on the course for what they called 'quality control' work. The ultimate goal is to ensure that caddies provide a valuable service to members. Caddies who did not make the grade had to retake the course. Only one retake is allowed.

I felt a little stress associated with the exam loop. That was exacerbated by a long drive to the course in stone silence. I finally erupted, having all this anxiety building inside. "What if I fuck up?" I cried out. "You won't," Glenn responded in the usual verbose manner. As I was about to get out of the car, I shouted, "Hey Glenn, any final words of wisdom?" not expecting to receive much response. His advice was short and straightforward. "Keep your eyes and ears open," he said. Thanks, Glenn, for those insightful words, I thought to myself.

The exam loop went much better than I expected. My golfer was pretty cool. He talked to me about his thoughts as he approached each shot. I started to walk when I needed to wait, and he held his hand up, instructing me to hold up.

I had one eventful highlight during the round. My golfer, while being extremely helpful, was struggling with his swing. Of course, I am not a golfer and have only watched successful golfers a few times. From little that I have gleaned, my golfer's swing seemed jerky. In a wild impulse, I said, "Mike, slow and smooth this time." Guess what. His next shot was perfect. So was the one after that. His entire round made a 180-degree turnaround. That was cool.

Mike gave me a glowing report and stated he would use me religiously once available. I won their 'TopGun' award, meaning I did not require a senior. I was elated. So was Glenn, although you would never know from his outward demeanor.

A drive home, I won't forget

After my class ended, we didn't hang around the Club long. We had dinner plans and needed to get back to the house. My tongue flapped like a flag in the wind as I described all the memorable moments during the exam loop. I was just about to enter my chant about "You da TopGun, you da man" when a policeman stopped traffic and directed us to an alternate route. Glenn seemed highly hesitant about going in that direction. He tried to back up and turn around, but traffic would not allow it. He eventually relented.

We drove down this road for approximately 5 miles when Glenn suddenly slowed to a crawl. I shouted, "Hey, Glenn, why are we slowing down?" I then noticed one of those crosses with flowers you commonly see just off the road on the right. This one had writing on it. It said, "We Love you, Abigail and Grayson". By this time, the car had stopped, and I looked at Glenn. He was crying. I said, "You know these people, don't you?". He didn't say a word. He spent a few moments composing himself and then drove on.

It was a sad drive back to the house. Glenn is a Stonewall in terms of projecting emotion, so this was a big deal. I hoped he would find it in his heart to open up about it, but he didn't initially.

We pulled into the driveway, and he stopped the car and said, "I need to tell you what that was all about. The names on that cross were my wife and son. About three years ago, they were coming back from a Junior Golf Tournament at East Lake when they were struck head-on by a 15-year-old who crossed over into their lane. The kid was not only driving a stolen truck without a license but was smoking a reefer. Abigail and Grayson died immediately. The 15-year-old died two days later."
"Whoa, Glenn," I said. I could not think of anything else to say.
.

We sat silently for at least 15 more seconds as Glenn's eyes welled for the 2nd time. He spoke again, "I have another thing I must tell you. Jack. This is hard to verbalize. Someday, if you marry and have children of your own, you may have some appreciation for the pain and sense of loss I have felt over these past three years. That isn't meant to discount or avoid painful events. Anyway, I have been trying to cope with the pain. I have tried pills and hydrating on Scotch. I tried dating. I have even volunteered. Nothing seemed to work. I would rather sit here in this house feeling sorry for myself. I decided to bring a teenage boy into my life, hoping that might fill in the void."

I sat for a short while again for what seemed like an eternity. To break the silence, I finally uttered something: "Wow. That is a lot to process." In my 16+ years on this earth, I have never been around someone I cared about who experienced a significant loss. I did not know what to say or how to act.

We walked inside; Glenn went into his chair and pulled his Scotch close by, suggesting more than one drink was in the offing. I went to my room, lay on the bed, and looked at the ceiling. So I am here to replace your lost son, as I thought to myself. How should I feel about that? I reflected a bit and then nodded off.

I was awoken a couple of hours later by a text for Rory. He said, "Sorry about what happened at your place. Hope your foster parent is OK. Do you want to hang out?". Part of me really wanted to bolt from all of this. I needed an escape…or so I thought. But from what? I have been using excuses to escape my entire life, and where has it gotten me? Until I got here, not a fucking thing.

Mostly, I've wanted to play the victim because I had a mother who didn't want me; Rory is a loser and just wants somebody to hang out with. Like the lapdog that just needs a lap. But, at the same time, he treats me with respect. That may be why I am drawn to him so much. I know he is a loser who gets me in trouble and drags me down with his poor me shit. The weird thing is that while my psyche feeds off the need to be respected by somebody, I know Rory is a loser, and that association makes me feel like a loser.

With Glenn, he doesn't give me a lot of respect. But whatever respect he does show, it is deserved. Somehow, that makes it better.

I texted Rory and told him, "Not tonight". I then walked downstairs to where Glenn was still sitting. I pulled up a chair in front of him and waited until he put his book down. I told him, "Glenn, you have been very good to me. Better than I deserved. I get that you had an incredible loss. If I can, in some way, help you forget about that loss, then I can live with that."

Glenn then did something that seemed totally out of character for him. He got out of his chair, came over to where I was, and hugged me. I can only count a few times where I've been hugged. I didn't know quite how to respond at first, but after a few seconds, I gradually hugged back with some emotional ferocity. After we had embraced for a moment, I told Glenn, "It will be OK."

Chapter 3

Golf, maybe something I am good at

School's Out

The 2nd half of my junior year at this new school was tough. I did not know anyone. I certainly didn't feel like I belonged. I wasn't classy or as refined as most guys. I was certainly nothing approaching a Southern gentleman. I'm a kid from a troubled past who faces a dubious future. In contrast, many kids here are fast-trackers to the Ivy League. I successfully avoided fights by keeping my head down and tending to my own business. There was one mix-up in the locker room—a little pushing and shoving. No punches were thrown. No blood.

As I sit in classes and look at all these other kids, I wonder if a high school diploma is even in the cards for me. I think when you are a foster child, you are assumed to be a loser or a dumb-shit. Many people don't quite get that when a kid lives in a state of chaos, things like studying and even concentrating are not givens. You are out late where sleep happens or doesn't. You come to class tired or ill-prepared, and the teacher bags on you. Being an outcast slowly chips away at your esteem. I have a lot of chips that need repairing, believe me. Glenn reminds me that I am intelligent and capable of excelling at school. I am not used to having someone believe in me. I hope I am worthy of Glenn's confidence.

Spring term was better. I cleaned up and have been working on shedding a lot of those mannerisms from the hood. Glenn helped with the wardrobe and constantly corrects me when I used those slangish mannerisms. I have made some new friends who were decent kids who avoided trouble. That needs to be my lane.

My grades were pretty good. Winter was around a C average, which was about what I was used to. I got Bs and Cs in the spring quarter, plus an A in American History. Not bad, Jack. Now, it is the end of my Junior year, and it is time to rethink some old notions of being a loser.

I connected casually with some guys on the school's golf team. They were impressed when I told them about my home course. That was stupid. I did not talk or dress like them. I am not a gentleman. I don't want to be one of them. I wasn't even honest. I wasn't even a golfer. "What the hell are you going, Jack?" I said to myself. In the middle of my guise, there were a couple of kids who probably wondered if I was making shit up. Still, I reflected on the golfer's lounge at the Club, where guys talk about their rounds and enjoy some quality brah time. I wanted that. I understand there is a community among golfers that makes sense. It will be interesting to see if I can develop those relationships more next school year.

Glenn asked me if I had any interest in playing spring sports. I told him I was historically small and slow. Back where I come from, I could not even pretend to have game. Posers get their asses kicked, I explained, so I always stayed in my lane and away from organized sports. I also told Glenn that being a caddie at the golf course was a good outlet and activity away from school.

Like sports, I told Glenn I probably did not have enough game for girls and dating. A big prerequisite was a car. Glenn promised to price-match me for anything I wanted to spend on a ride. If I can save $3000, he will throw in another $3000. That was generous. A bigger deal is the trust issue, Glenn says. Our last couple of months have been good, but I still have ways to overcome the...' sins of the past, as it were.
I still have my eye on the red-haired girl at the Club. A car may play an essential role in my courtship of that young hotty.

First Loops

It is 5 am on Saturday morning, and first sunlight peers through my bedroom window. I had a restless night. I had this strange dream where I was in the hood running. I was trying to figure out what I was running to or from. Perhaps I was running away from my past...or toward a better future. Maybe that is why dreams are so vague. Dreams give your brain a chance to interpret them the way you want.

It felt like I had barely gotten to sleep when Glenn's harsh, imposing voice abruptly awoke me. "Jack, get your ass up!" I lay there for a moment while I gathered my senses. Then it hit me. Shit! I had totally spaced out that I had a 6:30 loop at the Club with Chase Carson. This is a great loop, and he will drop me like a bag of dogship if I am not there. I can't be late.

I am throwing on my clothes, and Glen said, 'Jack, it is really simple. If you are going to be a caddie, there are just six simple words to remember from the first day of your caddie school.' I almost rudely interrupted him to stop his rant, "Glenn, I know, I know. Show up. Keep up. And Shut up!".

I grabbed a cup of coffee and a couple of power bars and jumped in the car, where Glenn hauled me out to the golf course.

Glenn came back to the Club to pick me up around five that afternoon, and even he could tell I had an unusual skip in my step. "Guess what, Glenn, I made $400 today," I told him with delight. "My most ever–by far." As I removed my loop uniform and put it into the trunk, I got in the car and started explaining my day.

Chase Carson, who is usually a dick, was having a monster day. He won a bunch of money on the front nine and was feeling pretty cocky, I thought. On the back, his game tailed off, but by then, he had started drinking and didn't care. He gave me a $200 tip and said, "You earned it, son." That felt good.

Glenn said, "Where did the rest come from?". I told him I had another loop in the afternoon. Jim, another looper, didn't like the guy he was looping for and gave it to me. "I think he just wanted to take the afternoon off if you ask me ." Glenn smiled as we headed home.

"Hey, Glenn," I said, trying to get his attention. "My afternoon loop was with a guy who knew you. I can't remember the guy's name, but he was also a lawyer who has had a few dust-ups with you over the years. The guy said you were a good lawyer." Glenn smiled and looked ahead. He muttered, "....a few dust-ups…hmmm".

Glenn generally didn't talk much about work unless there was a lesson for me. Just out of the blue, he comes forward about this case where a teenager breaks into this guy's storage shed where antique cars are stored. There had been multiple burglaries on this property, so the owner installed a gun with an automated release that would shoot anyone who broke through the door. So this teen breaks through the door, Glenn explains, gets blasted in the leg, and almost bleeds to death. The homeowner is arrested for assault and attempted murder, and then he calls me,

I asked naively, why did the homeowner get arrested? The kid was the one who broke in? Glenn explained that back in the 1800s, you could shoot horse thieves. Nowadays, you can't even use force to defend your property. You can hardly use force to protect yourself. The exception is if your life is threatened.

"That's crazy," I said. Glenn then explained with his Southern style that there is a lot of crazy stuff in the law these days. As a lawyer, you defend your client using the law you have. That is not much at times. I am going to have to work my butt off to keep this client out of significant jail time.

Then comes the civil suit.

"What's a civil suit?" I asked. Glenn responded, "It is when one side knows that they have you by the balls, and then they shake you down for everything they can." So I asked him if the kid who broke into the guy's shed was in line for a big parlay. Glen said, "Probably, but remember he also got shot up pretty bad, spent a week in the hospital, and could have died."

"Here is my lesson to you, son," Glenn said in this overly serious voice where the eyebrow dipped. "You get into people's business. You put yourself in places you don't belong. If you make bad choices, then bad stuff is going to happen. It is as true as moonlight, boy. It's the same as when I was your age. "

"I know you've dealt with a lot of bad shit in your life. I have, too, frankly. I am going to help you learn to make better choices. You've done better. I don't think you are sneaking out at night like before. I've told you this before. Once you realize your life is worth something, then you know it is stupid to squander it away or put it at needless risk. Life is precious." he said. He then got quiet in a strange way. I wondered if he was reflecting on how fate stole the lives of his family.

It was a hot evening, and Glenn threw a couple of steaks on the grill. We whipped up some grits and cornbread and quietly celebrated a good Saturday.

After dinner, I went inside and turned on a ball game. The Braves were playing. I'm not much of a ball fan, but I will check out the Atlanta teams. I could see Glenn sitting on the porch outside, smoking a cigar and enjoying a glass of Glenmorangie as usual. While he sat there, he would get this far-away look on his face. He was obviously deep in thought.

Later, my friend Rory texted me to see if I wanted to hang out tonight. For a moment, I reflected on Glenn's words as I watched him out on the porch. I told Rory, not tonight, dude, but I will take a raincheck, knowing that Rory's raincheck would likely remain an uncashed marker.

Church Sunday

Most Sundays, we go to Church. Glenn attends the Your Sins are Forgiven Baptist Church. He would never strike you as a church-goer, really. Glenn swears, drinks, and smokes cigars. He says, though, that the Church brings him peace. I imagine that is related to losing his wife and son, and I certainly know better than to give him a crap about something so personal. I just go and shut up.

I've got a loop today, so we are attending an 8 am service. I am not shy about saying Church was never my thing. Glenn said it wasn't his thing either, but said sometimes things happen in your life that change you. Glenn said, "God's hand will reach out to you whenever you are ready to accept it." Well, I don't know about any of that. I am just following the 'house rules' Glenn and I agreed upon when I moved in with him here six months ago.

After Church, we headed out to the Club. On the way out, Glenn was grumbling about something. Something in the sermon may have ticked him off. He is like that.
As we drove out, the thought hit me. I will be damn glad when I can drive myself. I asked Glenn, "Hey, Glenn, were you serious about the dollar match for the car?". He grumbled, "If I said it, I meant it". I told him I had saved about $2500 and was starting to look around. "It's gotta be reliable…and not a race car," Glenn said. "Got it, Glenn," I said and then put my face back in the cell phone. Glenn drove on.

He had a tee time at 10. I didn't have a scheduled loop and would hang out in the loop shed to see if anything opened up. During the downtime, I watch a little TV or yack with one of the other loopers in the shed. Today, Tim was there with me. He is my best friend among the loopers. He is also a regular golfer and always buggs me to come to his public course and play with him. I don't even own clubs, but I told him I would consider it.

Tim and I were watching the US Open. We could see the 1st tee area from our vantage in the shed. We were talking, then out walked the red-haired girl, Jen Laird. It was a hot day; she wore white shorts and a blue low-cut blouse. This gal is fine. In Glenn speak, he would call her a stunner. Unfortunately, she was not alone. She was playing with the guy I had seen around. He was a good golfer but struck me as one of those meathead types. That may be her type. If so, I am shit out of luck.

I figured she would be making the turn around 2, so she would be walking by in a couple of hours. Maybe I could casually cross paths with her about then to at least say hi. We watched the US Open to pass the time. At about 2, I positioned myself so that I was by the cart path as if I was waiting for something. As she walked toward me, I noticed the meathead guy was ahead of her, talking to someone. Jen noticed I was looking at her, and she smiled back. As she approached, I said, "Hi, a great day for golf." She stopped briefly and replied, "Yes, it is…maybe we should play sometime". She winked as she walked off to join up with the meathead guy. Wow, my mind was racing now.

After Glenn finished his round, we met at the Club, where I was jabbering about the Jen girl. My mouth had been going non-stop for about 10 minutes until Glenn finally held up his hand, which usually meant he wanted me to shut up. He said calmly, "A gentleman should focus the conversation of other people around him while being a good listener. Then you can talk about yourself." While I did not consider myself a gentleman, anything but one, actually. I understood his point. I needed to shut up.

Armed with new ways to conduct myself, I told Glenn in a formal southern tone, "Tell me of your exploits on the course today ."Glenn started to speak when one of the members in his 4-some from another table turned around and over-spoke him. He said, smiling. "Don't let Glenn tell you otherwise; he played with his pants on fire. That son of a bitch took everyone's money."

The unusually quiet Glenn launched into a 5-minute monologue describing his fantastic round as members of his foursome chimed in. It was fun, and I enjoyed the camaraderie. I was also moved by the way the other golfers showed me respect. In the past, I was commonly pissed on or the brunt of jokes. To have a Club member treat me as a gentleman was cool. It made me feel like I was starting to rise about that dark past. I was happy for Glenn. I was also pleased for me.

On the drive home, I told Glenn I thought I might like to try playing golf. He said, "Well, OK. ". Does that mean he supported the idea? There was a long pause, and then Glen responded, "Since you are not my legal child, I would have to acquire special dispensation from the Club for you to use the course. I do not view that as an obstacle. It would just take time. 30 to 60 days, I estimate. In the meantime, I would be happy to assist you there if you want lessons. I also have a spare set you can use until you establish your swing. After that, you will want a custom fitting that match the clubs to your swing.

"You need to know golf is not an inexpensive sport," Glenn uttered reluctantly. I sense that he wants to support my endeavor, which he thinks will benefit me. However, he had made it crystal clear that he is not an open checkbook and that I must participate in discretionary expenses. I told him that I understood and felt obligated to contribute. However, I wonder if Glenn would take my money.

Internally, I felt very gratified that Glenn supported me in learning golf. But there was a small matter I needed to address, but I felt hesitant, not knowing how Glenn would react. "Glenn, I was telling you about Jen Laird. She is not why I want to learn golf, but she is a factor. I don't want her to see me stink it up and wonder if I should start at another course for now". I said. Glenn countered, "Jack, I get your point. However, don't overthink things. Getting proper instruction is critical for a starting golfer. I highly recommend Jeff Langley, our teaching pro. He is the best around."
In my brief history with Glenn, I know that when he' highly recommends', it is code for 'you really should do what I recommend or else.' I said OK.

I was ashamed to tell Glenn why I wanted to start at Tim's course. At least at that course, if I looked like a chump, no one would care. Unfortunately, Glenn has taken that off the table. If I don't want the Club—or Jen—to see my crap game, I better shorten the learning curve. I will find YouTube videos of Bobby Jones, the world's best golfer, and see if I can duplicate what he does.

Starting a new endeavor like golf is forcing me to confront another reality. I am scared to death of failure. Sadly, failure and Jack Jeffers go together like peas and carrots. But it is all I've known for most of my life. Historically, I've been like the beaten dog who lays there motionless, expecting the whip to return even after the beating stops. I have spent my life lying there waiting for the next whipping.

But today was different. I am choosing to see myself in a new light. I start by telling the guy in the mirror, 'I am not a loser.' That negative shit has been dogging me my entire life. I sincerely want to be a person who can figure out a way to maybe rise above their shitty, tumultuous past. Glenn assures me I am not a dog that deserves the whip, referencing the whipped dog metaphor. I trust Glenn on many things, but as hard as I try, 16 years of negative programming is still going to be damn hard to rewrite.

Jack, the Golfer

Glenn told me I have a lesson with Jeff Langley next Monday. That is good. Monday is a non-loop day. In the meantime, I have been sitting in my bed watching Bobby Jones swing the golf club for what seems like a thousand times. There is no real reason for choosing Jones, except he is the only good golfer I know. I could have included Jordan Spieth, who I have watched several times.

I put the video on replay, and it just repeats over and over again. I even watched some videos describing the critical components of Jones's swing—things like balance, the takeaway, weight shift, straight left arm, and extended finish. There is a lot of stuff. While that plays, I visualize my body in my mind executing that motion. I see why Glenn was steering me toward an experienced Pro. As the problem was described, a golfer can't themself. A good instructor can see things you can't see or feel. Great instructors can explain and devise corrections when your swing is all messed up.

With my first lesson looming out at the Club, I needed to start swinging an actual golf club. I pulled out a driver and swung out in the backyard, doing nothing but visualizing the videos I had been watching over the past five days. I even took videos of me swinging and tried juxtaposing them next to Bobby. I tried looking at these from different angles. They could have come out better, but overall they were not bad. I find I am pretty comfortable working with technology and figuring things out. Jones swings much faster, even though it seems much slower....and smoother.

I had a loop Sunday with a four-handicap. I have learned that golf uses handicaps to measure ability based on your scoring history. A handicap of 12-18 is pretty average. A handicap of 4-11 is good. +2 - 3 are top club golfers. +3 and below are professionals. Jordan Spieth is like +9.

This golfer was good, don't get me wrong, but during the loop, I started seeing things in this golfer's swing that were counter to what those Bobby Jones videos show. This golfer bent his left arm some–not a lot–but enough to be visible. He also did not look right on his finish. Not sure why.

According to him, he finished with a one-over-par 73 and could have hit the ball much better and consistently. He played mainly from the rough but showed me many other ways to score in golf. From 50 yards in, this guy was money. It did not matter if he was under a tree, in a sand trap, or just chipping off the green. He found a way to get the ball in the cup. That aspect fascinated me. I have looped for guys who could bomb the ball, but when they found themselves in trouble, things would go to shit. It generally ruined their rounds.

After the loop, I told this guy I had never seen a short game like his before. I asked i he could share a few pointers.

He said his formula is pretty simple. You first assume that 75% of your practice time is spent on the short game. Next, make sure you learn sound fundamentals and practice good fundamentals. That's called learning technique. Then, you need to gain a special relationship with your short irons– almost a connection–such that those clubs become an extension of your arms and hands. They call that 'feel'. You need both. A golfer gains those with repetition, repetition, and more repetition.

Those words were powerful. I understood what Glenn was talking about when he described those with the gift of taking complicated concepts and making them understandable.

When I got home, I pulled out a pitching wedge and a handful of balls and went out in the backyard. The first ones were dribbles. I realized that a stiff left arm resulted in cleaner contact. Once I shortened the swing, I started getting a little pop in the shot. There was some good progress there.

My Monday lesson could not come soon enough. I was both scared and incredibly anxious with anticipation at the same time. I feel prepared for a beginner, however. Investing the time with the videos was a great idea. That seems to assuage much of my feelings of anxiety.

First Lesson

My lesson with Jeff Langley seemed to go well. Jeff was about my size. He swung in a similar form to mine. It was slow and smooth. He emphasized consistency and accuracy. Plus, I thought he was generally cool. Not arrogant in the least. He tried to find positives in all swings, even those that resulted in bad shots. "Those are the ones you learn from," he explained.

I told him about my recent loop where the guy shot 73 and stunk it up off the tee but was a master from 50 yards in. Jeff explained, "Working on all aspects of the game is essential. Many guys think they can show off their manhood by pounding 300+ drives. However, the game is won with accuracy, consistency, and a solid short game. "

I agree with Glenn that Jeff is very good at making complex muscular movements like you have in golf seem simple and understandable. I started out just with my swing. I then swung the Club while hitting the ball. My first shots were 10-yard dribbles. Almost instantly, a bunch of negative thoughts entered my brain. I thought to myself, "Stop it, Jack. You can do this.` With each swing after that, I steadily improved as Jeff offered instruction.

He pointed out a lot of subtleties. One of those was I gripped the Club like I was trying to choke a chicken's neck. He said instead, think about gripping the Club like you are holding a chick. The tension should be barely tight enough to keep the Club in place during the swing but loose enough that you don't hurt the chick. That made perfect sense. He also suggested less tension in my shoulders. We also discussed maintaining a connection between the Club and the body during the backswing. He showed me an excellent technique to determine whether my swing and body were connected.

I was hitting the ball pretty well by the end of the lesson. The last half dozen I hit were mostly in the fairways, around 200 yards. Of course, I am still determining if that is good. Jeff didn't give me much feedback initially but wanted to download it with Glenn afterward.

After the lesson, I was walking back to the clubhouse when Glenn arrived. He walked down to speak with Jeff to see how it all went. I was scared to death. Was he going to tell Glenn I was a loser and a colossal waste of time? I sat and waited pensively in anticipation.

Glenn walked up to me with his typical, sober, straight face. I always find him hard to read. In this case, his blank expression provided me with zero encouragement. He was like a poker player who was careful not to expose his cards. It became apparent I would have to wait for him to speak.

He ordered drinks as we sat in the lounge. He scooted his chair to the table as we waited and asked me how I thought it went. I told him I thought it was good. I like Jeff, and he explained things in a way I understood. Things improved following Jeff's instruction. I assume that is what you want." I said. I told Glenn, "Come 'on, I know you are just toying with me. The anticipation is killing me. You win. "He said, "OK, OK, here is what he said".

"Jeff said that he has been teaching golf for 20 years and has never seen a golfer with such a natural swing. Some golfers take years of instruction and cannot execute what Jack already does after just 1 lesson. It was quite extraordinary, to be honest." he said. He added that a kid with a swing and natural ability is only half the equation. As you know, Glenn, golf is a game of nuances, and it takes time and practice to master those. That said, the sky's the limit for this kid. "

Glenn asked me how I felt about all of that. I told him I was shocked. It is tough for me to imagine actually being good at something. At the same time, "Golf just seems to come very easy for me," I told Glenn. "Well, it doesn't come easy for me, Jack," Glenn uttered. We just laughed, and we enjoyed dinner.

When I didn't have scheduled loops, I was either in the backyard working on my short game or at the public course playing with Tim. Glenn appeared to be all-in on my golf game. He had a big backyard and helped set up a green and pin area. Glenn also bought golf mats that I could hit off and not trash his grass. He had agreed to let me remove some of the yard to install a putting green made out of some new astroturf-like material. We are talking about putting in a sand trap, but that may have to wait until we finish the other projects in the queue. What we have now is an incredibly short game set-up. Jeff says 75% of your practice should be on your short game. You can now practice at the house any time you want. 50 yards in.

I really like building things. I have little knowledge or background in doing things, but I can watch YouTube videos and learn what I need to know. I tell Glenn all the time, "Technology is your friend. Embrace it." He grumbles.

One other thing. The other day was my birthday, and Glenn came home with a birthday cake. I had to be honest and tell him that this was the first birthday cake I had ever had. It had a big happy 17th on it. He then sang "Happy Birthday" to me. His singing stunk, but I appreciated the gesture. Then he came out with a present. It was a very elaborate launch monitor. These devices tell you how far your ball goes and in which direction based on the ball's spin coming off the clubface as you hit it. It also gives you a lot of key performance measurements about your swing angle that is not discernible to the eye. From those, you can refine your swing even more.

This thing costs about five grand. I told Glenn this is way too much. Maybe he might use the opportunity to discuss how this gift symbolizes our growing relationship or how much I meant to him. No, he used one of his short canned expressions. "I can afford it," he said.

Glenn made my day special like no one has ever done before. His singing "Happy Birthday" moved me so much that I even got a little misty. I have never been recognized personally like that before, and I almost do not know how to act when things center on me. I wanted to tell Glenn I loved him for everything he had done for me, but I didn't know how. I just put my arms around his shoulder and said, "Thank you. I appreciate all you did".

I played a half dozen rounds at the public course by late September. My first score was 92, but my last score was 78. Tim is a consistent low-80s golfer who has played most of his life. He calls my progress nothing short of miraculous.

I had a couple more lessons with Jeff, but he said there was nothing else he could do to improve my swing. He put my swing on his golf swing monitor that, like mine, also showed swing analytics like distance, club head speed, and angle of attack. He didn't explain what that means, but he said it is incredible that the monitor shows that each of your swings are practically identical. "I've never seen that, even among championship golfers," Jeff commented.

He went on to say, "You just need to spend more time on the course," he said. Glenn suggested he could help me with nuances. Meaning, learning what to do when the ball is above your feet. What to do when the ball is below your feet. How to hit out of deep grass. Stuff like that. We also had a club fitting. Jeff gave me a great deal on a new set of Titleist clubs, previously a demo set.

Club Junior Golf Championship

I had pared my loop schedule down to only one or two loops a week; those were my loyal clients. It felt a little awkward being a looper at the same time as I was a member…of sorts. Finally, this last week, Glenn was given a letter by the Club stating that I could not loop and be a playing member at the same time. I decided to hang up my loop uniform and go over the loop shed to say goodbye to some of the guys. As I was walking out, Tim asked me if I was playing in the Club's Junior Club Championship in two weeks. I said, "Of course not. I am not ready for competitive golf." "Bullshit!" he said. He told me that if I play in it, he will loop me..for free. "OK," I said. "I will think about it."

I talked to Glenn as we were making dinner together. I told him, "Something tells me I should do it, but frankly, I am scared to make my game public." Glenn then added, "Are you saying you are scared of failure?" "Probably," I said with a tone that suggested my position was weak. Glenn said, "I cannot tell you what to do, but I can give you advice my father gave me once.

"If you don't go after what you want, you will never have it."
"If you don't ask, the answer is always no."
"If you don't take a step, you will never move forward."

After much skillful prodding from Glenn and Jeff, I finally put my name down to play in the Junior Championship. Tim was adamant about wanting to caddie for me. I told him I didn't want to embarrass myself in front of a friend. But he quickly convinced me his experience would be invaluable.

In my play so far, I was playing good shots. However, I was still learning nuances. Tim reminds me that golf has a 3rd dimension—the mental portion. Tim explains the mental game involves mostly decision-making and knowing what a smart play and a poor percentage play are. In the brief period I've been playing–even as a looper–I have seen numerous types of people. Some, as Glenn says, "come unglued" during the heat of battle. A caddie can really help you keep your head on straight and 'stay present,' as Tim likes to say. I was convinced.

Tim proved his metal on hole three during the tournament's opening day. I had hit a great tee shot, but a tree limb partially blocked my approach to the green. I pulled out a 3-iron, planning to keep the approach under the limb. Tim grabbed me and said, "You might be able to make that shot, but if you hit the tree limb, your ball will likely fall in the hazard, and you might be looking at a big score." He told me the smart play was to punch out somewhere to the right of the green. That takes the hazard out of play. I took his advice and hit a solid five iron right of the tree limb, leaving me a 20-yard shot over the trap to the green, which I got up and down for a par.

The rest of the day went very well. Actually, it was far better than I had ever expected. I had played steady from the fairways and avoided big mistakes. I finished with a 73, which was my lowest score ever. That put me in the final group for Sunday. Interestingly, one of those players was the meathead kid playing with Jen Laird that day. I had not seen Jen at the Club but wondered if she might show up.

For the Sunday round, they rolled the greens, making them incredibly fast. The pins were also in challenging locations. They called it "US Open" conditions. A much larger gallery had assembled for this round. Glenn and Jeff were there to watch me. So was Jen. She looked amazing. Knowing my infatuation with her, Tim repeatedly reminded me to focus on the course. She had my mind wandering for sure.

During the final round, I was playing solidly. I took a stupid double bogey on seven after hitting my tee shot behind a tree. My punch shot then went across the green and into the hazard. I got a bogey on the next hole after having a buried lie in the sand. I did follow that up with a birdie on par 5, ninth hole, to finish at 38. I was four shots behind at that point and was starting to press to catch up. Tim reminded me to focus on my game and stay present. That is, focus on the shot in front of you, not on your score or the ones behind you.

I did a decent job keeping my head in the game during the 2nd nine. I have to admit, it was hard with Jen staring at me. A couple of times, my mind wandered, wondering what she might be thinking rather than what shot I needed to make. Also, there were members of the Club barking out "beautiful swing Jack" all the time, which started getting to me. That notion of having a good swing crossed my mind against the objective of scoring well. It is like the pretty boy who is an airhead, a dick, or a dipshit all in one. People focus on one glowing trait but overlook the overall person. Obviously, I was clearly doing too much thinking.

I hit the ball well on the 2nd nine, the best I have in the tournament. That wasn't enough. However, I was ultimately done in by the tricky greens. I had been practicing on our new putting green in the backyard, which is very nice but extremely slow. These greens today were like putting on concrete. And that was no joke. I carded a 40, which gave me a respectable 78. The winner beat me by eight strokes. At least the meathead kid didn't beat me. I kicked myself inside over the ones I let slip as golfers commonly do.

Glenn told me afterward, "3rd place. Well done, Jack". A few moments later, Jen approached me and said, "You have only been playing for a couple of months. You are amazing! She then said, "Call me sometime," and handed me her phone number. Afterward, I was beaming from ear to ear. As I lamented to Tim, that phone number may have been the tournament's biggest prize.

Chapter 4

Jack takes his game to high school

Senior Year in High School

The school had been in session for nearly a month before the Club's Junior tournament, and for the most part, it had been pretty ho-hum. There were mostly the same people, teachers, and classrooms. Going in, there were a lot of reasons to feel this year would be a repeat of last year. But there was something astonishingly different after the Junior Club Championship.

Apparently, Joe Carlson, the winner of the Club Junior tournament, is a cousin of Calvin Carlson, who is on our Johns Creek High School golf team. Joe told Calvin about this incredible golfer named Jack Jeffers who attends there. He has only played a few months and shot a 73 on a challenging lay-out. "He has a swing that is as smooth as silk," Joe told Calvin.

Now, the entire school golf team wants to be my friend. On some level, that is a bit bothersome. That is, the ordinary Jack is not worth shit, but the golfer Jack is somehow worthy of their friendship. I talked to Glenn about it, and he told me not to read too much into that kind of stuff. Use it to help you achieve your goals. I told Glenn, from where I come from, you didn't have goals. Glenn said, "Your golf can take you a long way if you want. It is not too early to start thinking about college and what you might want to do afterward". I nodded. Thinking about college is undoubtedly a new thought for me.

One thing I learned from my challenged upbringing was knowing how to be humble. Glenn talks a lot about the 'golf gods' as if they are real people running things. "They are fickle," he says. "They can be merciless. They steal opportunity exploiting your greatest weakness. They side with the hidden flaw." He had a long list of idioms. Anyway, while getting props from kids over a single round of golf, I realize I have not accomplished anything. It is on me to keep working, learning, and improving. That's what Jeff, my coach, says. He agrees with Glenn that the golf gods are fickle. "Keep working, stick to the process, and don't overthink your score. "Jeff says. "With young golfers, results come and go. Expect that. The golf gods are no match for the golfer that is prepared."

One of the side benefits of being in the golf group at school is being exposed to a new class of people. My first reaction is that these are not necessarily my people. Most of these kids are what I would have called 'rich bitches' who have parents with money. They are all members of country clubs who were given Mercedes on their 16th birthdays. Before getting caught up in much here, I must remember to stay in my lane.

I am a foster child just one year from living in Juvie Hall. I see sunlight ahead, but the demons of my past are not far behind.

Golf season does not officially get underway for another two months, but most team guys play year-round. Last year's team captain, Eddie Crosby, approached me and said that his stepdad belongs at East Lake and they can get us on and asked me to join their 3-some to make a 4th. Without thinking, I told them I would play.

East Lake

East Lake is among the region's oldest and most prestigious golf courses. It was the home course of the infamous Bobby Jones. I am looking forward to playing there tomorrow.

Last week, the Atlanta area experienced heavy rainstorms. So heavy that they even submerged my putting green in the back yard. Glenn mentioned that it appears there is a drainage issue in that area of the house, builders had failed to address. I decided to take it upon myself to fix this for him. The solution involved digging and filling a 40-foot trench with gravel that would connect this section to the main drainage line on the side of the house. Some gravel was delivered on the side of the house, and I spent the evening digging a 2-foot trench and filling it with gravel. Glenn likes to have jobs left orderly, so I hauled the remainder of the gravel back behind the shed to avoid an unsightly pile. When I was done, my body was tired, and it ached.

I'm a kid where bumps and bruises wear off quickly. I had hoped to feel OK before playing tomorrow, but no. I was worse. Before getting picked up to play at East Lake, I expected to stretch and get my body right. Again, no luck. When I arrived at the range, I could tell with the first swing that I was having trouble with my follow-through, which threw everything off. The round reflected my achy body and was a disaster. I shot an 87, which is very pedestrian for even a high school golfer. To make matters worse, the guys I played with were total dicks. They were jeering me and making smirks when I made a bad shot. They even tried to get in my head to disrupt my putting. I expected a little comradery since we would be on the same team next year. But instead, once they sized me up as a poser, I became fresh meat and more of a pissing post than a comrade.

"You know what bothered me more than playing like crap?" I posed rhetorically to Glenn, "was the way these guys shit on me. I thought I was their friend. They made me feel like a fucking loser."

After some frank discussion with Glenn, I find myself relieved. All the pressure associated with living up to their lofty expectations is gone. Glenn, who is never short on the philosophy of life, says, "You learn more from your failures than you do your successes." "Very true, Glenn. I said, "I learned a hell of a lot today."

That evening, I called Jen Laird for the first time. It's not a knock on Glenn, but he is anything but nurturing. He will listen, spew a little philosophy, but then pick up his scotch and put his head back into his book. I wanted to call Jen, thinking she might bring me some needed solace. She did.

We chatted for at least 2 hours, and our talk was easygoing and fun. At first, I was very hesitant to share my rough past. I was worried Jen might think of me as a bad kid or a loser. But it turned out she respected how I overcame my struggles and was on a path to improving my life. I told her I was still a work in progress, but Glenn was helping me a lot. Jen shared that she had lived with her grandma, Isla since her parents died when she was young. Her grandpa also passed away five years ago. They lived in a fancy part of Brookhaven, not far from the Club. She attends a private school close to there. My golf game blew her away. "You are obviously a natural," she said. We agreed to get out and play together next weekend.

Admittedly, I only have a little experience interacting with girls—two or three phone calls. No dates. Not one kiss. I guess that qualifies me as a newb. Still, my less-than-experienced self felt a connection to Jen.

Even as I was conversing with her, I couldn't help but notice her alluring southern charm that could make, as they say, butter melt in your mouth. When the situation calls for it, she can easily command a room with her presence. She exudes warmth and sensitivity yet possesses remarkable strength. Her confidence and self-assuredness are apparent, and she never comes across as critical or judgemental. I cannot help but notice how she genuinely seems interested in me as a person, a rare quality that I have seldom experienced. She appears to see something special in me, though I'm unsure what that is. I'm eagerly looking forward to seeing where this relationship goes.

Is there a flaw? No. She is perfect. Even Glenn likes her.

My return to school after the Saturday debacle at East Lake made me feel defensive. I have obviously lost stature with the golf group. I am sure they see me as a poser, but that is OK.

That isn't going to make me jump off a bridge or anything. Yet, I did enjoy talking golf with them and hanging out even though they were shallow and arrogant. I am better off without them. Jen agrees.

New Car

I have been saving my money from loops for a few months now. I had to first pay Glenn the $1500 for the damages he incurred over that Rory incident. Since then, I have accumulated another $5000. As part of Glenn's agreement with the Club, I could not loop in and be a playing member at the same time. Instead, I have been providing playing lessons. Members pay me to play a round with them. I give them playing tips and swing instructions along the way. That is better than looping. Plus, it pays better.

Glenn was generally supportive of the car idea. He is probably tired of all the chauffeur services he has provided me. He agreed to match my contribution, which was a great help. I had been looking at cars over the Internet and showed some to Glenn that might work. Glenn was pushing me toward a used Jeep Cherokee that a Club member owned. He argued that the Club member would not sell another member a lemon. He would likely stand behind the car if it went wack. "Buying from a used car lot or a private citizen is always a crapshoot," Jack suggests. I was OK with the Jeep. I also knew that Glenn's support was valuable. I went with Glenn's suggestion. He also agreed to pay for the insurance. That's a great deal.

I got my driver's license a few days later. I can't wait to get out on the road by myself.

I would have been shocked if Glenn had sent me off in a car where I go anywhere or do anything. As anticipated, Glenn first needed his paternal lecture before he felt comfortable turning me loose. Glenn reminded me that I was still on a somewhat short leash. He pulled out our contract and said you have committed to me, and I expect you to honor it. I told Glenn, "I know. You can trust me". I think he knew I meant it.

I got another text from Rory later that night, wanting to hang out. He had been texting me regularly, but I ignored him, hoping he would disappear. This text had a second sentence. "Answer your text, asshole."

I took my first solo trip to the Club in my Jeep. I had a morning lesson with Jeff and would meet Jen in the afternoon to play a few holes.

With hesitancy I told Jeff about my catastrophe at East Lake. I hated exposing my failure. Jeff has taken a personal interest in my development. I wonder how he will respond. Will he see it as a personal setback? I was surprised by his response. He told me not to read too much in it. Think of it as a blessing to help you become a better golfer. "Every error or mistake is an important learning opportunity," Jeff said. He strongly suggested that I keep a journal to record my journey.

He checked out my swing and thought I still had that silky, fluid motion that was my signature. I told him I watch Bobby Jones videos to dial in my swing. He said, "I knew I had seen that swing before but could not quite place it. Bobby Jones. Of course."

He provided me with a few significant tips. According to him, being a golfer is similar to being any other type of athlete. One must take care of their body by regularly stretching, lifting weights if possible, and staying physically fit. Additionally, it is essential to refrain from engaging in activities that may harm the shoulders, back, knees, or feet. Currently, you stand at around 6'1" and weigh 160 pounds. In my opinion, you could build a little more muscle. Assuming you do not grow, 180 pounds might be your ideal.

After the conclusion of the lesson, Jeff then sat down with me in chairs inside his teaching area. He wanted to make sure we were on the same page regarding my future goals and plans. He said, "We agree that our goal should be to point toward a strong senior season of high school golf. I don't think it is out of the question where you could earn a college scholarship at a major university." I responded with astonishment, "Jeff, get outta here! I'm still a hack compared to lots of the guys out there." Jeff then said, "Maybe today, but you have to look at the trajectory of your progress. They are here", using a flat arm to indicate a limited growth curve. "You are on this path." angling his arm steeply upward. "I think college golf is very realistic for you."

After my lesson, I always tried to get in some more work to reinforce what I learned. While hitting, my mind kept wandering toward thoughts of college. My wiring told me college was not an option for people like me. Glenn has mentioned it. That is still a lot for me to wrap my head around.

I was really looking forward to my afternoon golf date with Jen. I was on the putting green, waiting for her to arrive. When I looked over at her walking toward me, my heart just melted. I was not ready to expose to her what I was feeling inside. "Hi"

is all I could get out, at least displaying a big smile. She said with her warm southern style, "Hope you brought your A-game today. You'll need it". I laughed. Usually, my afternoon practice play is like a business trip where I work on shots and try different things. Today's play was like a peaceful afternoon stroll. We played a little golf, we walked, we talked.
Afterward, we enjoyed some food at the lounge. It was getting toward dusk when I dropped her off at her car. Before she got in, she reached over and kissed me softly. My head was spinning as I danced toward my Jeep.

On the ride back home, I reflected a lot on the day. My brain focused mainly on the kiss, but hormones were taking my thoughts in lots of directions. "She's actually a pretty good golfer." I mused. I have only seen a few women play. Most were clumsy and lame. Jen's swing is decent; surprisingly, she can bang it out there for someone not particularly big. I was impressed overall. I spent a lot of time watching her golf mechanics. It was more like being enamored with watching her body in action.

I also spent some time observing her demeanor. Jen had fun on the course. She didn't rattle, She didn't throw clubs. Jen doesn't swear. She was easygoing, fun-loving, and highly competitive, which I liked. She missed a short put, which would have given her a birdie 4 to beat me. She got this angry, frustrated expression that demonstrated how much winning mattered to her. As they say, she was kicking herself inside but then could let it go. I liked that.

Glenn has told me you can tell a lot about people by how they conduct themselves on the golf course. He said how people deal with competition, frustration, success, and failure are very similar to how they deal with life. "Golf is the game of life,"

Glenn says. I bet he read that somewhere. The more I play, especially as I watch Jen play, the more I see the parallels.

Golfing episode with Glenn

Glen and I golfed very infrequently. I'm not sure why that is, although I think Glenn primarily views golf as a vehicle to enjoy a social experience with his friends. He didn't like to practice. He also didn't comment much on how he performed. He just saw my compulsion to improve as incongruent with how he views the game.

It was an unexpectedly sunny Saturday afternoon. Earlier, Glenn had been working in the yard, and he said that his friend Roger called and he was going out to the golf course. I said, "Do you mind if I join." He said, "Sure," probably thinking I was going to practice. He seemed somewhat surprised when I showed up with them on the 1st tee, ready to go.

Glenn started out uneasy but eventually settled in. He said afterward that this was probably the best he had played in a few years. He scored an 80, which is pretty good for a 15 handicap. He attributed it to being able to watch me. Glenn said, "Normally, I can be very quick between the backswing and the beginning of the downswing. Watching your silky smooth swing helps me with my transition."

I viewed the afternoon as more of the practice round and not trying to score. Roger had to leave early. I used that to practice some shots I do not usually practice. For example, I was sitting on the right side of the fairway, about 155 yards away. That is a comfortable 8-iron for me. I then dropped a ball to see if I could muscle up a 9-ron. I then grabbed a six-iron to know if I could lay off some to achieve a 'knock-down' shot, where you use the lower trajectory club to minimize the wind. I am playing low-70s golf, but I see a lot of areas where I need to improve. Glenn said my swing has never looked better.

After the round, we did what we usually do: sit on the Club patio, relax, and have beverages, followed by food. I usually had an Arnold Palmer, a combination of iced tea and lemonade. Glenn drank different things, but it was a Tanqueray and Tonic today. I took a sip and thought it was nasty.

We ordered food and were sitting there, and Glenn said to me, "Son." When he called me son, it usually meant he had something important to say. He said, "Son, I've got something to share that I don't like to talk about but think you should know. "He grabbed his drink with two hands and held it in front of him as he spoke.

He said, "My son Grayson and I played golf together often. It was where we went for one-on-one, father-son bonding time. He was a strong golfer. Not nearly as good as you, but good. After his death, I constantly reflected on our times together on the course, and for a long while, being out here made me feel empty. One particularly tough day, I threw my clubs in a dumpster, vowing never to play again. I think that was my way of punishing myself as I anguished over my loss." Glenn got teary-eyed and even shuttered some as he spoke in a rare emotional moment. He has never spoken of his son previously. Was it rude or heatless of me to never inquire or bring him up? I don't know. But Glenn is private. He does things his way at his own pace. I doubt he faults me.

Glenn explained, "I used to go to the 1st tee and just sit there and reflect. I would sometimes walk the course and replay our various interactions. Eventually, I realized that I needed to move on with life. I bought clubs and started playing again. This catharsis, I will call it, coincided with you coming to live at my house. I have played golf all my life. I played with my grandfather. I played with my dad, like I played with Grayson, and have now played here with you. I realized just today that, aside from family, golf is my anchor. It has stood the test of time and is part of my identity. In a funny way, it is part of my gift to you."

Glenn grabbed his napkin and wiped his eyes. This was one of those moments where I should have hugged him or said something showing appropriate empathy. Instead, I grabbed his hand and said, "I appreciate you sharing that with me." I still felt odd about how my role evolved in his horrific story. But at the same time, I am incredibly grateful for the lease on life he has given me.

Thanksgiving dinner between the Andrews and the Lairds

During my upbringing, holiday events were always a mixed bag. They were generally an afterthought. It was sometimes a ceasefire from the tension-riddled environment. Glenn is not a guy who gets festive during holidays. He is not decorating pumpkins or putting out corn stalks. In fairness, Thanksgiving is a family event; with Glenn's family gone, there could be painful memories. Jen reminded me of that. Still, Jen invited Glenn and me over to her house for Thanksgiving. She lives with her grandma Isla, and there would be just the 4 of us. Glenn was adamantly against it initially but finally relented to avoid appearing rude.

I met Isla once while she was at the Club. She seems a few years older than Glenn, but not much. I thought she was attractive for an older woman. She struck me as well-educated and classy, and it is obvious where Jen gets her qualities of poise and strength. These traits are clearly passed down. I wondered if Isla might be someone who could energize Glenn's love light. Jen, I discussed it several times. However, Glenn is not my real parent. Thoughts of him in romantic settings were creepy.

Glenn and I showed up with a bottle of wine—Glenn said it was expensive—along with our favorite casserole. The dinner was terrific, at least to me. It was like those epic Thanksgiving feasts you see in movies. We had turkey, dressing, mashed potatoes, salads, and Glenn's killer casserole. We enjoyed some apple pies for dessert that I couldn't get enough of. Glenn is not known for being talkative. Yet, I did catch him in casual conversation with Isla. He even smiled, avoided all the 4-letter expletives, and was incredibly well-mannered. Both Isla and Jen called him a real gentleman.

On the drive home, I was dying to ask Glenn if he saw a potential love connection. Glenn will say no and will argue he was just being polite. Glenn's wife has been gone for three years. Isla's husband has been gone for five years. Jen and I agree that it is time for both to find love again. At the same time, the loss of loved ones is a personal thing that we should stay out of. Jen agreed… sort of. She thought that perhaps they needed a little push. "That can't hurt much," she said. I responded, "I don't know if Glenn will respond well to nudges.."

Christmas Break at TPC Sawgrass

A few days later, Jen and I sat at the corner coffee shop, reminiscing about the Thanksgiving dinner. While drinking coffee, Jen turned to me and said, "You know what we should do? We should plan a Christmas trip to Florida." After pausing momentarily, she said, "How about TPC Sawgrass in Jacksonville!"

I raised my eyebrows, intrigued by the idea. Then I broke out, "That's a great idea! We could play golf, enjoy the beach, and spend quality time together." I then turned and said, "Glenn is never going to go for it." Jen responded, "We just need to work on him a little." demonstrating her assertive side. "I know Isla will go. I wonder if maybe Glenn has a little spark for Isla that just needs a match. Let's give it a try," she said.

The next day, we pitched the idea to Glenn. "TPC Sawgrass is so much more than just a golf course," I said. "There is a camp there I would love to attend. David Leadbetter teaches it. It's a beautiful resort with exceptional amenities. We could do so many things there. The beach is close. Jen then chimed in, "The Florida sun sounds fantastic. Plus, it's the perfect place to relax and recharge after a hectic year. "

We were not expecting him to be thrilled. We saw his body language, which generally means pushback. He then surprised me. "Let me think about it," he said. I knew better than to poke the bear and waited for him to respond. A couple of days later, he surprised me again. "You know what, Jack?" he said. That trip to Florida over Christmas sounds fun. Let's do it." I just about fell over in my chair with that one. "Wow." I thought. I could not wait to call Jen.

The trip turned out to be everything I had hoped for and more. Jen and I had a blast playing at TPC Sawgrass. The course was badass, just as I anticipated. My favorite moment was when we both hit nice shots onto the island green. I two-putted for par, but then Jen rolled in a nice 20-footer to beat me with a birdie. She must have jumped a mile in the air. Later, I attended a 4-hour camp on advanced short-game techniques. David Leadbetter taught it. This guy knew his stuff and was a great teacher. I learned a lot.

But the biggest surprise was the development of Glenn and Isla's relationship. They had been a little friendly–mostly polite–at Thanksgiving, but their relationship seemed to blossom this week. They took walks along the beach together, shared meals, and even sneaked in some kisses when they thought nobody was watching.

Jen and I were thrilled to see our plan come to fruition. As we packed our bags and headed back home, we knew this trip had succeeded in more ways than one. "Mission accomplished" as we high-fived each other.

Glenn and Isla's relationship was not the only one that blossomed, however. Jen and I also took a big step forward. We had a lot of memorable moments. I watched our relationship transform into a romantic couple before my eyes, almost like I watched it in a movie. She owns my heart. I think own hers, too.

Disrespect at School

After a quiet, relaxing holiday, it can be a shock to the system to return to school with all the hustle-bustle. I dropped my books off at my locker and was weaving through the hallway full of kids. I walked by the golf group, who routinely hung out in their usual corner. One of them said to me as I walked by, "Hey Jack-off, how's that slice?" referring to my lousy slice during my East Lake debacle. The other kids just smirked.

In my old life, I was used to getting dissed–aka insulted– frequently for one thing or another. This insult felt completely different, though. It hit me at my core. I had not thought about golf in this way before, but I suddenly realized that this is much more than a game to me. It has become part of my identity. It was like when a kid insults your mother. The diss was personal.

Historically, when you are dissed, you only have about two seconds to craft a suitable comeback. In those cases, the comebacks were ones I had heard repeatedly over the years. In anticipation, I kept a hundred canned responses in my hip pocket that I could access immediately. Even with the most clever canned responses, your likelihood of saving face was still no better than 50-50. In this case, I was blindsided, unable to create even a single countershot to fire.

Rather than embarrassing myself by shooting from the hip, I wisely walked by without adding fuel to the fire. Later, Glenn and I discussed it, and he offered strong words of wisdom. In his curt, pithy tone, he said," You were disrespected. Get over it. You will not gain respect back with your mouth; you can only do it with your golf clubs." That is a very different approach from what I learned in Shitsville. Posturing was almost as important as winning. After I reflected on it, I agree that Glenn's approach is the better strategy.

After Glenn's comments and some reflection, a sort of explosion went off inside me that said Jack, be determined to prove them wrong. I sprang out of the chair with a newfound mental clarity that I admit had been lacking for a while. I grabbed my clubs and went outside to start practicing. Golf season begins in about a month. I will employ every ounce of energy I have to ensure I bring my best game. I am leaving nothing on the table. That is my new mission.

High School Golf Season Starts

I must admit, I have been waiting for this day for quite a while. The Club Junior Championship last fall was great, but I left a lot on the table, as they say. The East Lake round with the golf team was a resounding disaster but maybe an essential wake-up call. I learned that I can't show up and expect good things to happen. According to Jeff, hard work has to be my hallmark if I want to reach my potential. I am still learning the game. "Feed your passion," Glenn says with another bit of his concise and nearly profound philosophy.

When I was on my way to the office to pick up my grade, I walked past the golf group in the hall this morning, I got the usual smirks, snickers and jabs. I would have taken that stuff personally a month ago, but that is rolling off of me now. I smile. Glenn was right, and I have realized that I will never earn these guys—or anyone else's—respect with my mouth. The only place I can do that is out on the course. These guys want to take me off my game by getting into my head. I am not going to let that happen.

To add to the insult, the school paper had extensively previewed the upcoming golf season. I was reading it as I waited in line to receive my grades. The school has a storied tradition of being among the better golf high schools in Georgia. The spread in the school paper had write-ups about the returning stars. To no one's surprise, there was zero mention of me.

My grades for last semester finally arrived and I opened the envelope with anticipation. Admittedly, my academic history was never overly impressive, making these envelope openings mostly painful events. For most of my life I was a disengaged student who did not give a shit. At the same time, I always knew I wasn't an idiot. Glenn, to his credit, is changing my thinking.

I slowly pulled the card out and looked with amazement. I immediately had to text Jen. "Guess what? I got 4 A's and 2 B's, including an A in Physics and Advanced Math. Not bad for a kid from Shitsville. Jen, with her usual positivity, responded. "Jack, I knew you could do it." She followed that with a red heart emoji.

The good news on the grade front put me in an excellent mood for tryouts at the nearby St Marlo Country Club that afternoon. I had been anxious about it, but that anxiety yielded to confidence as I approached the Country Club from the highway. Glenn tells me your confidence level is directly proportional to your level of preparation. I was indeed prepared.

I walked out to the practice range carrying my clubs on my shoulder. Many kids nowadays use pushcarts, but I chose to carry. I noticed golf group members huddled around the practice tees, cracking jokes. I was off by myself, minding my own business. I sensed a heightened focus and determination. During the round, I was all business. I did not joke or interact with the guys. I did not even talk, for that matter. Instead, I let my game do the talking, as Glenn suggested. I shot an astonishing 63, equalling the course record. That was eight strokes better than the next-best player.

Following the round, they post your score on the board for everyone to see. Moments after my score went up, the buzz around the clubhouse was almost deafening. There were multiple high-fives and congratulations from the coach and the pros at the Club. In a particularly sweet moment, the golf group greeted me with excitement and seemed anxious to re-enlist me into their group. "Hey dude, come over and tell us about your round." one of the members said. As I walked toward them, I was highly conflicted between joining in the conversation and regaining that comradery or giving them the finger and a little payback for the way they shit on me. I opted for payback. I just walked by, turned my head, and said back to the group, "Hey, I think I got that slice figured out." They all knew exactly what that meant.

That round was a great springboard into the first half of the golf season. I was named team captain, much to the chagrin of several teammates. I was worthy of that designation by being the medalist in each of the first five tournaments. Our team also won 4 out of those five tournaments, mostly riding my coattails. Most of my teammates were cool and genuine. One guy, in particular, came across as a jealous dick who was chafed that I stolen his spotlight.

For a short while, I got caught up in my own press. I was admittedly enjoying giving the finger to the golf group for how they shit on me initially. However, as time passed, I began to rise about the pettiness and absorb the enormity of the experience.

The Masters

Jen and I thought taking a few days off from the tournament schedule was much-needed relief, especially after the constant grind of practice and travel. I'm looking forward to setting my clubs down for a few days.

A while back, Glenn suggested that we attend the Masters golf tournament for a few days, not knowing that Isa and Jen would also join us. Luckily, Glenn had a family friend who's a principal in the Masters organization, and he kindly arranged our tickets and accommodations.

I have not followed professional golf. I have seen a few tournaments on TV at the Club, but I only know a few players, except the infamous Bobby Jones and maybe Jordan Spieth. I am following more, however.

It still blows me away as I observe how Glenn and Isla have become an item. He kicked and screamed against meeting this gal, and now they are practically joined at the hip. They've even had hookups. Personally, that creeps me out a little. I realize Glenn is not my actual parent. Still, older people having sex is not the best visual for me. Four of us in two rooms in Augusta will be a little odd, but something tells me this will be fun. I'm sure of it.

As we are loading up, Glenn asks me if I can drive. "You're the better navigator," he says. Actually, I was thinking to myself that he wants to get a little in the back seat. Jen would have jabbed me in the ribs if I mentioned that. She is far more refined in that way. What it really is, I think Jen is mindful of giving Isla the utmost respect. Casual joking or poking fun is not within the nature of their relationship.

We arrived at our place in Augusta at about 8 pm. I unloaded the gear, and Glenn informed me that he and Isla would turn in early.

"OMG," I say to Jen as she almost bursts inside with a look halfway between a blush and a grin. "Jen, don't you see a lot of irony here," I said. "For years, Isla kept you caged up away from horny guys. But when given the chance, she struts like a dog in heat." Jen said in her sultry southern voice, "I think it's kinda cute."

I told Jen, "I've got a special treat for you." "You are going to introduce me to the back seat of your Lincoln," she utters in her sexy, southern voice. I responded, "No, something better…well, almost." I then pointed down the street to the Waffle House.

As we walked toward the iconic building, Jen told him she had never been. "Come on," I said. "Really? "I then reflected for a moment on her upbringing in stark contrast to mine. It gave me pause. Before we walked in, I was trying to explain that these places were much more than a spot for a basic breakfast anytime, day or night. "No, it is much more than that. It is a cultural experience," I explained. She was still looking at me as if I was speaking in Chinese and seemed totally clueless with what I was saying. As we walked in the front door, I suddenly stopped. "These are places where my people go," I exclaimed, extending and waving my arm across the horizon to welcome the community of friends.

As we walked to sit down, we saw people with diverse ethnic origins. You saw blue-collar working people. You also saw a booth of thuggish looking kids who were hanging out. Over in the corner was what looked like a businessman in a suit. The waitress comes over and says, "What will y'all have?". We ordered some waffles, eggs, and grits. The food was fast and basic, as you would expect. Jen ate without saying much.

After we left, we went for a walk downtown. I would not call the area rough but more akin to I've always called working-family modest. Jen was noticeably quiet. That often means she is either uncomfortable, being polite or just reflecting. In fairness, I gave her a lot to reflect upon. She has only known me as a golfer, a country club type of guy. She did not know the tough, inner-city kid who slung drugs and fought with police. During those times, the Waffle House was like home.

Jen and I walked for at least 10 minutes in total silence. There was a domestic dispute across the street, with loud voices going back and forth. I said, "Maybe we should go back," then she said, "I'm OK." I could tell she wanted to say something but didn't quite know where to start. I got very anxious at that moment, not knowing what direction this conversation was headed. Was she going to tell me she couldn't date thugs or that she did not belong here?

Jen then started talking. I expected this was going to be important. "In the six months or so we've been dating, I realized I have only known Jack Jeffers, the high school golf phenom, Jack Jeffers, the family member of an old southern aristocrat. I did not know the abandoned Jack, who lived over yonder in Shitsville and had to fight for survival. Grams warned me that 'rolling stones like you can be hard to stop,' which I get. At the same time, I am deeply drawn to you in ways that don't make sense. I realized once I walked inside the Waffle House that there are parts of you that I don't know. But I am falling in love with you, Jack Jeffers and that includes all of you, both the good and bad. I understand Isla, your history and lack of family raises red flags. Still, I can see past that. My momma wrote in a book once, that when you follow your heart, happiness will follow you too." she said. "Well, my heart says yes to Jack Jeffers and that includes the whole you."

We stopped walking, and I turned to her and kissed her passionately. I then told her I loved her…for the very first time. I knew at that moment that this was the person I wanted to spend the rest of my life with. We returned to where we were staying and had an incredibly intimate night together. It was one I will likely never forget.

I woke up at about 6 to the sound of Glenn rattling around the kitchen. He was standing at the coffee machine, putting on a pot of water. I told him jokingly, "You're lookin' awfully spry this morning…ya ole hound dog." Glenn just smiled in a way you could tell he knew I had exposed his carnal experience from the previous evening. At the same time, you could tell he was a little proud of himself, even though he wouldn't tip his hand. I thought to myself. This is probably what the happy Glenn is like. He seems content and carefree. There were not the usual sneers or dower expressions. He just seemed totally unimpeded as he mulled about the kitchen like the world was his.

He threw some sausages into the pan, started cooking…, and whistled.

After breakfast, we were off for an incredible day at Augusta National. We started out touring the clubhouse and the neighboring grounds. The pictures and memorabilia of Bobby Jones and many others who had played there over the years were simply spellbinding. I explained to Jen that a person who wins the Masters golf tournament becomes a Green Jacket Club member. Each member is invited to play this Master event throughout their lives. She said, "Maybe that will be you someday."   I thought to myself, "Ya right."

We watched the players perform during the tourney for most of the day. I was amazed at the consistency of the tough shots players were making. We followed Jordan Spieth for a few holes. As we looked on, he hit a laser from the woods onto the green. He hit within a few feet from a fairway bunker. He also hit an eight iron over a row of trees to give himself a makeable putt for birdie.   I thought to myself, these are the shots I don't have that I need to master.

As I reflected on what I saw, I shared some thoughts with Glenn. "I don't think I have these shots in my bag," I responded.   Glenn responded with something that resonated. "Remember Jack, Jordan has been playing golf since he was a little kid. As you gain more experience, you will add shots to your repertoire. Be patient."

We watched players making shot after shot. My head was racing. At the same time, as they hit, I could see myself on the fairway executing pin-point approaches and various other shots around the green. I thought to myself, maybe Jen was right, that I could be here someday". That may represent fantasy or a lofty goal. A lot of people think this is possible for me. I may need to start listening to them.

Golf Season continues

After the high from Masters, I am instantly reminded of the big tournament in a week, a smaller tune-up match a few days later, and Districts. My game has been firing on all cylinders, and I can't let up now. The word of the day is practice, practice, and more practice.

The Tommy Thomas Invitational is an annual high school golf tournament held in Columbus, Georgia. It's a big deal because the best teams in the State compete. It should be a tough challenge. I'm feeling nervous but also excited to play against top-notch competition. To date, I have not been seriously challenged. That should change soon.

Columbus, Georgia, is out in the western part of the State. Unlike the State tournament, the golf team typically budgets for one trip a year. We will leave a few days early to take on the Fields Country Club in LaGrange. That's where this year's State championship is held. I want to get experience on that course ahead of State. We're stoked for the tournament and can't wait to show off our golf skills!

Fields Country Club was pristine. I was approaching it more as a practice session than one where I was trying to put up a score. A couple of the guys were crowing about beating me. "Whatever," I said to myself. I am saving my powder for the Columbia tourney on Sunday.

The Saturday before the Tommy Thomas Invitational was scheduled as a down day. A couple of guys were going to go hang out at the mall. A couple of others wanted to go fishing on the Chattahoochee. I went to the golf course to work on my short game and a few other shots that needed work.

That practice turned out to be worth the effort. On the first day of the Invitational, winds were swirling, and greens in regulation were anything but a given. My short game was spot-on and saved me from sure bogies several times. I was elated with my 67, given the conditions. I didn't play my best golf but cobbled together a strong round. I was tied for the lead after the first day. Good!. The team did not fare well, finishing in the middle of the pack. Andy, our number 2 golfer, carded a poor 78. Afterward, he complained about this, that, and the other. I jabbed him for not choosing to practice the previous day, "At least you caught yourself a bass." I quipped.

I was paired with the two other leading golfers on the second day. These two guys were clearly the best golfers I have ever played against and probably two of the best in Georgia. One came in 2nd in State last year and has already accepted a scholarship to play at the University of Georgia in Athens. The second guy was 5th in State last year but has been on a terror lately. He holds offers from Augusta State and Tennessee-Chattanooga.

I learned something early in the round. Playing against top competition improves my focus. We all wanted to win badly, and every shot mattered. After the first nine, we played well and remained tied at three under for the day. On the back nine, the winds really came up. It turned out my low, piercing drive fared much better than the two others who were big bombers. I played from the fairway while they struggled with sand and trees. I added an exclamation point to the round with an eagle on the par five 17th. I finished the back with a five-under 30 for a 63, winning by an impressive six strokes.

I was walking on cloud nine after turning in my scorecard. Golfers and coaches approached me, giving me high-fives and looking forward to watching me at State. I was chatting with my coach when the head coach at Georgia Tech showed up and gave me his card. He said, "I think you've got the stuff we need at Tech. We also play in Alpharetta, a very nice course near home." Later that day, I got visits from Alabama, Florida State and Clemson. My coach told me you were great today. Expect a lot more college interest.

The following week or so, the buzz I generated from that win was mind-blowing. Recruiters from all over the country were calling; I became an instant celebrity at school and even got an interview from a writer at the Atlanta Journal-Constitution. From my perspective, this all feels premature. I won a few tournaments but haven't earned anything yet. Still, the notoriety was gratifying, although I have yet to come to grips with the notion that I am worthy of the attention.

The following Sunday, the sports section's front page featured my picture with the headline "High School Golf Phenom Rises from Tough Inner-city Past." The article featured my accomplishments, especially my big win last weekend. But most of the article was about my arrests, time in juvie, and various brush-ups with the police. The article spent a lot of time on me being a ward of the foster care system and wondered how someone could transition from loser to phenom in just one year.

I felt very crappy about all of that dirty laundry coming out. I considered much of that private stuff that I did not want out in public, especially with all the kids on the golf team and at school. Glenn says there is a lesson there for how much to say to reporters. "Reporters are like opposing trial lawyers," he said as he looked straight into my eyes. "They come across like your friend, but they know how to use that trust to manipulate you. Remember one thing: they are only there to advance their own interests. That's important." I feel bad that I may have embarrassed Glenn, whose reputation was probably damaged by the article.

I called Jen later on and asked her what she thought. She said, "There is a biblical passage that applies. And 'they will know the truth, and the truth will set you free.' She explains that this means that now that the truth is out, you are no longer held hostage by having to keep secrets. Jen was pretty active in the Baptist Church and seems to have learned her lessons well. At the same time, I gotta praise her wisdom. She was spot-on. It did feel like the truth had set me free. Freedom felt good.

District Championships

The 4 of us got together for Easter. Glenn has me in church pretty regularly. I acknowledge that is his thing, and I am here primarily there as a matter of respect. He says it brings him peace. Given what he has been through, I get it. I sit and listen. I am not particularly engaged with the biblical stuff, but

I buy into the moral lessons. Love one another. Be good to your neighbor. I'm all in on that. The biggest motivator right now is sharing with Jen. Religion is part of her life, and I need to share this with her. Hopefully, I can figure out all this religious stuff for myself at some point.

After church, we all met at the Club for a big Easter brunch. It was extremely fancy, with shrimp, crab, prime rib, standard breakfast stuff, and exotic desserts. This fancy dress-up event thing is not really my scene. You can tell that it is Isla's, however. She is very refined and classy, with perfect manners. Jen is definitely cut out of that cloth. At the same time, she is cool and appreciates basic things. Jen can also be a little edgy. That is, she can operate outside of that refined box when she needs to. She can sometimes swear, joke with the boys, and be aggressive or even commanding. I like that.

After brunch, Glenn and Isla went home and did whatever it is they do. Jen elbows me if I cringe over suggesting what that might entail. We decided to head to the Club and play nine holes. This was the last chance I had to get out on the course before Districts, and I had some things I wanted to work on. During this practice play, I will target shots. I hit specific places on the course to experience different circumstances. If my shot is not what I like, I may drop a ball and hit another. Jen plays her one ball where it lies. She indulges me as I practice. I think she senses my anxiety in advance of this important tournament.

The two-day District Championship this year is at Capital City Country Club in Brookhaven, a course I have played multiple times. It is among the older courses in the area in an established, wealthy community with large estates. That is where Jen and Isla also live. It is also home to tougher neighborhoods where you would not venture out alone. I warn Jen frequently.

There was a lot of buzz surrounding this tournament compared to the others I have played in. Being close to Atlanta probably played a factor. Jen says they are here to see you. "I don't know about all that," I said in an attempt to stay humble. Still, I could not help but notice the gallery size that was following our group compared to others.

I was thrilled with the first day. This Peachtree Course is the older of the two courses at Capital City. It has narrow, tree-lined fairways with imposing bunkers and challenging greens. I do not try to overpower the ball like many guys out here. It is definitely a manhood thing to hit the shit out of the ball. I sometimes give up a lot of yards to some of those hardbodies I like to call them. I jest about how a lot of guys play more with their dicks, than they do their brains. I leave emotions like ego and testing my manhood at home. My game is accuracy, consistency, and playing smart. This course fits my game very well.

I finished day one with a five-under 65; I led by two. I feel good about where I am but a little frustrated due to the number of strokes I left on the table. As sharp as I was from tee to green, my putting was off today. Fortunately, Jeff Langley, my instructor from the Club, was there and agreed to take a look at what I was doing. That helped a lot.

For Day 1, there were maybe a hundred people in the gallery. Day 2 had double that. "This is crazy!." shouted the golf coach. He routinely gives me a pet talk before the round. He says essentially the same thing each time. He says, "Play your game, and you will be fine."

I started out shaky with rare bogies on number 1 and 2. I felt a little rattled. At those times, I must admit, self-doubt starts creeping in. More than once, I reflected back to the horrendous round at East Lake. The rest of the nine was a battle where I had to scramble for par after par. I finished with birdies 8 and 9 to finish even par for the round. That helped ease some tension. "Stop the bleeding," as they commonly say. My opponent from Norcross, who trailed by 2, caught me and was actually leading by 1.

Usually, golfers, even in high school, are gentlemen and play with courtesy. This guy was a real shithead. Sure, some guys may try to get into your head to distract you from what you are doing. But they do it subtly with courtesy. This guy was neither subtle nor courteous. The funny thing was he didn't get into my head with his remarks. He did it with his rudeness.

As we were walking to the 10th tee, my looper friend Tim Shay came up to me and said, "This guy has a reputation for being an ass, tune him out. Rise about it. See it for what it is. Play your game."

Tim has a way of saying the right thing to me at the right time. Thanks to him, I came to the second nine more focused and determined. The gallery had grown appreciably, and there was a lot of commotion and movement in the gallery. Even as we were hitting, people—mostly high schoolers from other schools—were chatting, taking videos, and doing what kids do. By this time, Tim had me laser-focused and dialed in.

I birdied 11 and 12 with precise shots off the tee and a good club selection. My opponent from Norcross bogeyed 10 and 11. Then, on 12, he made a risky play. He tried to bomb his teeshot over the frees and onto the green for a birdie or an eagle. Instead, the ball nicked a tree limb and fell into a hopeless location in a hazard. He added to his misery by trying to push a bad position. Rather than take his medicine, he succumbed to the pressure of the moment and tried to get out of trouble. His ball crossed the fairway and landed in a creek. He ended up taking a quadruple bogey eight, which ended any aspirations he had of a championship.

Knowing my key challenger was history, I stayed in my lane and avoided excessive risk-taking. I avoided disaster on 13, where I had to hit backward 40 yards to get the ball in the fairway. I then hit a nine iron 150 yards over a tree, landed with 8 feet, and made my putt for par. I tallied birdies 15, 16, and 17. On the tough par five 18th, I creamed my driver and hit probably the most miraculous shot of my short career. I holed out my 22-degree hybrid from 210 yards for a double-eagle 2.

As I walked off the green on 18, a giant sense of relief came over me. Jen came up and gave me a huge hug, knowing that I had won. My 28 on back nine tied the course record. The 62 close left me winning by 11. As I looked out over the course and realized what I had accomplished, a feeling came over me as my eyes welled up. Jack, I thought to myself. Not bad for a guy who is only a year and a half removed from a jail cell.

The next couple hours were abuzz with reporters, photo ops, and high-fives. I was still in a state of euphoria, frankly. There was also the cadre of college recruiters giving me cards and shaking my hand. Things eventually quieted, and we decided to catch dinner outside the lounge. We invited Tim along as well. His input between rounds was crucial, plus he and I have developed a kinship that allows me to call him my 'best friend.'

Jen asked me at the table if I got a card from Vanderbilt. I started thumbing through the cards, and then she said, "Maybe we could go there together. That's where Grams wants me to go." I did not realize then that Isla and her late husband were law graduates there. "Yes, here it is," I said, alluding to the notion that Vandy might be a possibility.

We are walking together out to our respective cars. It is about dusk, and most people have left, except the cart crew moving equipment indoors for the evening. We were saying our final goodbyes to each other when this kid in a hoodie walked up to me and then pulled out a pistol and pointed right at my head. It was Rory. For a brief instant, I could see my life pass in front of me.

Rory said in a kind of hood slang I recognized, "Jack, golf phenom, my ass:" as he recited the headlines from the paper. The anxiety in his voice suggested he was probably high and in a state of distress. "You think you are hot shit with your golf trophies and your money. But you aren't shit. In fact, you're a piece of shit who forgot about your people. You pissed, no, you shit on them." Rory's voice starts to crackle, then breaks out in a full cry, "Jack, I thought we were friends."

I was petrified but knew I had to try to defuse things in any way possible. Glenn and Isla, about 15 feet away, grabbed one another and huddled together. I cried in a voice that made a veiled attempt at empathy, "Rory, we are friends.

Let's sit down and talk about it. Put down the gun, Rory". Rory replied, "You are not my fucking friend. You got hooked up with some fat cat lawyer, and then you threw me out like hot garbage". In a tone that is almost begging, I tell Rory, "Please, dude, put down the gun!" Before I would finish, Rory replies, "In the hood, we waste disrespectful fucks like you." In the next instance, I move to get in front of Jen to make sure she is behind me.

While Rory was talking, Tim had been subtly maneuvering behind Rory. Tim dives at his gun arm as Rory raises his arm to fire. The gun goes off, striking me in the right leg. I immediately collapse under the pain while Tim and Rory wrestle on the ground. Tim is fighting with Rory to gain control of the gun. Rory is not particularly big, but deceptively strong for his size. Tim, who is about my size, is using all his weight to desperately keep Rory's gun hand from getting free. At the same time, Rory is punching Tim in the face. I reached over and grabbed ahold of Rory's legs as I could tell I was bleeding profusely. Just then, a half dozen more shots ring out from the gun as Tim and Rory wrestle. I get hit in the knee and take another bullet in the side.

OMG is really the only emotion I felt at this tense moment. Thankfully, kids from the ground crew heard the gunshots and ran toward the skirmish. One of them stood on the gun to temporarily secure the weapon. The other kid was big and was able to subdue Rory physically. I heard sirens in the background, and that was the last thing I remembered.

Before the ambulance could arrive, I was bleeding heavily and ultimately fell into a coma. My next recollection was waking up in a hospital bed feeling dizzy and disoriented. A doctor was hovering over me with a bright light shining in my eyes.

"How are you feeling?" he asked as he looked under each eyelid. "Very groggy," I responded. "You have been in a coma," he told me as he moved his evaluation from my face to my leg. "You took gunshots to the upper thigh of your leg and into your knee. You also were shot in your side. You lost a lot of blood. The bullet in your leg grazed your femoral artery, and for a time, we were not sure if we could save your leg.

"How long have I been here?" I asked. The doctor said about two weeks.

About then, I turned to my left, and Jen was sitting in the chair next to me. As I acknowledged her, she got up and grabbed my hand. Jen was sobbing visibly. I asked her if she was OK. She nodded while continuing to sob. I was too out of it to know what to ask. She was about to speak when the doctor interceded. "Let's let Jack get some rest." She squeezed my hand and said, "We can talk later."

Later that evening, when I woke up again, Jen was there by my side. She seemed a bit more composed than earlier in the day. She stood up, grabbed my hand, and said with a quivering voice, "There is something I need to tell you. Glenn is in the ICU with a shot to the chest that grazed his heart. Grams is gone.", referring to Isla. Jen then broke out in a colossal cry I had never seen from her. With tears running down her face, I grabbed her and held her close while still trying to absorb the shock of what she just told me. I was still very foggy following the coma. I responded clumsily, telling her, "I am so sorry." I realized at that moment that there was probably nothing in the world that I could say to ease her pain. My hugs and sharing tears were perhaps the best medicine I could offer her at the time.

The following day, the medical team was putting on a new, more permanent bandage. Jen was at my side, as always. Tim stuck his nose in my room a few minutes later and asked me how I was getting along. I responded, "I've been better." I looked at him intensely, wanting to communicate something important. I said, "Dude, I am pretty groggy with all the dope and shit. When I get my head clear, I want to talk to you about what happened. But, in the meantime, I need to at least thank you for saving our lives." grabbing Jen's hand. "I owe you." Tim said, "You would do the same for me." He was about to speak more when the doctor came in and interjected. He said, "Good news. Glenn has been taken out of ICU. We expect him to recover fully." All of us responded with relief and gratitude. Tim replied, "I need to run, but I will catch up with you soon. Get well".

I doubt Tim realized at the time what a tall mountain that would be.

Chapter 5

Mending

Several days later, they thought I was well enough to leave. Jen came by and drove me home in a wheelchair, along with a lot of bandages and pills. My right leg feels very lifeless. I am currently lacking the ability to put any weight on it. Jen says it feels too lonely to stay in her house in Brookhaven and asked if she could stay with me for now. Isla's sister drove up from Macon to help with the funeral arrangements. That should help. Glenn will be coming home tomorrow. I expect Glenn to be heavily bandaged around his chest.

I have not said much to Glenn. I assume he knows about Isla. He is speaking some, but that dower expression I have come to associate with his sadness has returned. What do you say to someone who lost their family in a car accident and then loses maybe the love of his life in a shooting? Plus, it is my fault. In her sympathetic but pragmatic voice, Jen tries to convince me that this wasn't my fault." You didn't pull the trigger." she explains. I tell her I know, but my relationship with Rory brought all this darkness upon us. I said, "I might as well have pulled it."

Glenn came home on Sunday, also in a wheelchair. He can walk but gingerly. We have hardly spoken since the shooting. His sadness weighs heavily on my mind. As I watched him as he sat in his chair, I could not help but think what he had lost...because of me.

I sat there next to Glenn, probably looking pensive. I think Glenn may have sensed my anxiety over how to talk to him about Isla. He finally said, "Jack, I know Isla is gone". I said, "Glenn, I am so sorry. I know she meant a lot to you." "Probably more than you know," Glenn said. "For a while, I thought I may have gotten my life back. Then boom. All I can say is that God must really hate me." knowing that he didn't really mean that with tears running down his face.

"I see this as my fault," I told Glenn. "I did what we agreed. I shut off communicating with Rory, but obviously, that made him angry." Glenn then surprised me with his response. "Jack, this was my fault. It was mine. Do you hear me? I heard what Rory said out there, and it was obvious you heard my lesson about being judged by the company you keep. You were keeping your part of the bargain. I didn't anticipate this. No one could". As Glenn finished, I felt a sense of calm come over me. Jen and Glenn finally convinced me that Rory was an angry, jealous, and disturbed kid, and it wasn't my fault he was there. Glenn also told me, "You did not pull the trigger on the gun. ". He was right.

The Funeral

Isla's funeral was several days later. I had never been to a funeral before. It was a highly somber event. I was shocked by how many people attended. I assume these people Isla knew or were related to in some way. They also must have thought highly of her. I told Jen, feeling very awkward now, that Isla must have been very lucky to have so many who love her. Glenn made it there, although he elected to remain in his wheelchair. I sat with Jen and held her hand. She did not say much or show much. She seemed numb to it all, which was to be expected I guess.

I would characterize the ceremony as being much like a Sunday Church service, except they had people talk about Isla. I learned a lot that I didn't know. Isla's great grandparents were from Scotland. They were interested in the Scotch industry and formed a regional distributorship that sold Scottish spirits to bars and restaurants in the Southeast US. The company began just after Prohibition ended. Isla went to Vanderbilt and met James at school, and they were married shortly after graduation. James took over the daily operation of the distributorship and ran it until his death five or so years ago. Isla has a sister but no other living relatives. She was 64.

They had what is called a closed casket' where you do not see the individual in repose. There was a burial service at the cemetery and then a 'celebration of life' buffet at the Club. Glenn asked me if I could arrange a drive home. I think he got tired. I certainly did. I was trying to negotiate my way around without a wheelchair, using crutches. That was still a lot of work. I still needed a lot of help getting in and out of the car. This injury sucks.

The next day was scheduled for the reading of the Grams will. Jen asked Glenn to assist her. Glenn initially advised against it because he felt he was too close to both parties in the transaction. Jen argued that she needed someone of impeccable character, but moreover, someone she could trust. He was the only option. Glenn later agreed. I asked him after he came home from the reading. "Hey, Glenn. How did the reading of the will go?" He said "None of your business."

Two more weeks transpired without seeing or talking to Jen, and the wait was excruciating. In addition to that, I can hardly stand or walk. Glenn clanks around. We are in a total funk around here without an end in sight. Glenn urges me to give Jen distance to let her heal. My imagination can't help but think her Aunt may be somehow undermining our relationship. I am trying to focus on the positives. It is also a good time to get caught up in schoolwork. Glenn has been 'mobility challenged' and says he needs my help, even though I am unable to offer much given my own challenges. Part of me wonders if he wants to make me grovel, doing penance as he says. It is also possible that he is trying to get me off of my butt. Either way, I will cut him slack.

Front and center in my mind is that shit head Rory, for doing this to us. Fuck you! I hope you rot in prison.

Until now, I have avoided the press clippings and news reporting covering the shooting. Being home with time, I considered looking through the articles covering what happened that day. I have also wondered what happened to Rory. For the time being, I am not ready to go there.

Golf also feels way off my radar. It has been two weeks since the State tournament in LaGrange, Ga. I have not heard at all from the golf team. That feels strange but not overly surprising, given our history.

Something else that felt strange was when I returned to school. I am still in crutches, probably for at least another month. People may be uncomfortable worrying if they will say the right thing. I would. The reality is Rory took a lot from Glenn, Jen, and me. Nothing they can say will undo that.

People were generally cool. Most said, "Great Championship". Some said, "Sorry for your loss". I was OK with it all. I walked by where the golf group hangs, and they invited me over. I didn't know they had dedicated that State tournament to my family and me. I was moved. I didn't think they gave a rats about me, frankly. I was wrong. I asked about their State tournament, and they came in 4th. Pretty damn impressive if you ask me.

Until that day, golf had fallen off my radar. I was not thinking about my tournaments or championships. I also needed to consider my future golf career, certainly not college golf. Just getting beyond my mental funk needs to be job one. The golf group, my nemesis all year, were unlikely saviors.

When I got home, I grabbed all these recruiting letters, accumulating them in my room. Now, I am unsure where I want to go with golf—if anywhere. I was curious about how coaches looked at my accident and whether they still had interest after my storied past was exposed.

Most schools responded with something to the fact that they will be watching the summer tourney schedule. Keep them apprised. Walk-on opportunities may exist. There were only two schools that expressed unconditional confidence in my game. Georgia Tech and Augusta University (formerly Augusta State). I value loyalty, and both schools have scored with me in that regard.

Graduation came a couple of weeks later. It felt like it was a big deal. Glenn treated it like it was a big deal. There was a long period in my life when I wondered if a high school diploma would ever be in my future. I finished the Spring semester with 4 As and 2Bs again. Glenn congratulated me for the awesome performance. I thought to myself, that was pretty damn awesome, given the distraction of golf and the shooting.

When we got home, Glenn handed me a card. Glenn said, "I have a hard time expressing this. But my pride in your achievement goes beyond words." Inside the card was a check for $50K. I said, "Glenn, I can't take this." Glenn said, "You will need it to pursue your career in golf and get through college. You have shown me you can be responsible with money. I do not need to tell you to spend it wisely. I know you will." I responded, "Glenn, you have done so much for me already." Glenn said something profound: "Don't discount what you have done for me, son." "Thank you, Glenn." was all I could say, but it was not nearly enough.

Glenn had previously asked me what I wanted for the Graduation meal. I told him BBQ. Glenn turned me on to smoking meats a while back. When traveling, we are always seeking out select BBQ locations. We talk to experts and experiment with different rubs and grilling methods. It is a science but more of a journey we share. For our dinner tonight, we agreed on smoked brisket. I started smoking last night. It is generally about a 12-18 hour process. I am also planning to grill a little salmon as a secondary option. Glenn is great with mashed potatoes and is making his famous beet salad, which I love.

Tim and his girlfriend also came over and just arrived.

I was out on the patio slicing brisket. Glenn was serving drinks and setting the table when he heard a voice say, "Can you set one more?". It's Jen.

Jen had been pretty MIA for the past month. Once I saw her, my heart melted inside. All of my being wanted to reach out to her and kiss her. At the same time, I knew I needed to maintain some distance and not put her in an uncomfortable situation.

I greeted her with a polite hug. "Hi, Jack," she muttered, showing equal politeness. As we greeted, I ached to know the status of our relationship. Did she come as a friendly gesture to Glenn and me, or had she undergone some catharsis and had re-evaluated her position? That was unquestionably the elephant in the room right now.

The conversation at the table was casual. The brisket came out great, but my mind was not on the BBQ but on our formal conversation, like when you have guests who hardly know one another. Tim talked about looping at the Club. "We miss you in the loop shed," he remarked while trying to make casual conversation. He spoke about how he had been looping for Chase Carson, one of my favorite clients from last year. "Carson asked about you and how you were doing. He also wanted to talk about…what happened that night. I couldn't go there. Carson is a bit of an ass…but he pays well. " Tim said as the mood turned a little more somber.

Realizing the conversation was heading down a painful path, Tim quickly changed the topic. "How's the leg doing? Jack." "The gunshot tore my quad muscle up pretty bad," I replied.

They took the big bandage off last week. I can walk a little, but I still need a cane. It is getting stronger, but I will need a lot more time."

Jen, feeling the need to become part of the conversation, asked Glenn, "How is your rehab coming?" Glenn responded, "Getting back to normal." he said without providing much detail. "It will be a while before I can swing a golf club." "Fortunately, Jack helps me around the house as best he can. The neighbors have been helpful also." Glenn said.

The conversation then turned toward a more personal, sensitive topic. Tim asks, "Jack, have you given any thought to college or college golf?" I responded with a tone of indefiniteness, "College is in my plans, I think. I am taking the SAT exams next month. I chat with recruiters here and there. But, given the nature of my injury, they are guarded about whether I can regain my pre-injury form. Most want to see me back in competition before offering. A couple of schools have stuck with me unconditionally. They say they will offer once I can show I am academically qualified." I responded. "I value loyalty." glancing up subtly at Jen.

Glenn asked Jen, "Have you given any thoughts about college?". She replies, "My parents and my grandparents are Vandy alums. It was always in the plans for me to follow in their footsteps. At the same time, I now own a spirits distributorship. I also need to put Gram's house up for sale. My Aunt wants to stay there, but I feel It is too big and lonely for me."

We finished our meals and then adjourned to the living room for dessert and coffee. For me, the mood was upbeat yet somber. I still needed to have a greater sense of the status of our relationship or if there was even a relationship. Tim and his girl got up to leave, thanking Glenn and me for the great meal. They offered final congratulations on my graduation, then left. Jen then got up and seemed to be heading toward the door. She then took an unexpected turn. She said, "Jack, could we chat?".

We walked out to the patio and sat down across from one another. Jen had a very reserved tone and demeanor that made me think she had carefully scripted her thoughts.

She then utters, looking mostly down, "Jack, this last month has been extremely hard for me. I know it has probably been just as hard on you. I also know my silence has made me seem unfair and cruel. The shootings and the loss of Grams have changed me." She pauses for a second, trying to keep her emotions under control. "Before the shooting, my life was perfect. I had a loving boyfriend with an exciting future ahead. I also had the loving family anchor and the support of a caring grandmother. Now that she is gone, so is my anchor. I've become like a ship adrift, not knowing where I am going or where I will end up. To further complicate my life, I have also inherited the family distributorship company that needs help." I wanted to respond, but Jen interrupted and said, please let me finish. "In that one instance (referring to the shooting), I changed from being a carefree, sassy teenage girl to being a woman responsible for maintaining the family legacy with a full plate of responsibility. And I am not sure if we are the same couple who fell in love with one another." She paused, sounding relieved to finally get that out and gesturing that it was my turn to respond.

I was dazed, trying to process everything Jen said. I then asked 'Do you fault me for Gram's death?" She said, "No. My

Aunt does, however. And that became an issue between us. I accepted that you are on a life journey that unfortunately involved a seedy past. But I came to accept that the seedy past was….in the past and was not who you are." I asked, "It sounds like your Aunt is not my friend. How does she fit into the picture?" The short answer Jen gave was, "She is not in the picture. I soon figured out that she was playing me. And that her goal was to move into the house and take over Grams's role in the company. She contends that it is her birthright."

Jen said, "I found some letters between Grams and her dad. At the time, her dad had terminal cancer and needed someone to take over the business. Grams, a recent 24-year-old Vandy graduate, was living in Charleston with her new husband, James. Teresa, the Aunt, left home as a teenager many years earlier. She joined a 60's stoner band, The Grateful Dead, as a groupie and married some hippie she met along the tour. While Teresa was off getting stoned, Grams and her husband James uprooted their lives and moved to Atlanta to be with her dad and fill-in the void at the business. Years later, Teresa reappears and thinks she could move into a prominent role after Grams and James built a life around the business. Once I discovered Aunt Teresa had an agenda, I told her she needed to leave."

I then asked Jen what had been on my mind all evening. "Where do we go from here?" I asked. Jen responded in a soft, caring voice. "I still am not sure, Jack. "she said. "I am unsure if our paths align or if we want the same things. I still care about you," as her lip quivered, I could see a tear stream down her face. "Why don't you call me in a couple of weeks so we can chat." I told her in a somewhat relieved voice, "OK." At least we would be talking, I thought.

After she left, I spent the next couple of hours lying on my bed, staring at the ceiling. All I could think of was my life and Jen, wondering what the futures holds.

Jack Rediscovers Game

It has been almost six weeks since the accident. My wound is healing well, but walking is still a challenge. My doctor suggested that I probably have experienced some muscle atrophy due to lack of use. He strongly encouraged me to get into physical therapy, which should a weight-lifting regimen to regain my strength.

The Club employs a licensed physical trainer and rehab specialist. I've made an appointment to see her. I desperately need to get myl body working again.

Upon arriving in my Jeep for the appointment, I stepped out with my cane and opened the trunk, juggling my golf bag and the cane simultaneously. Out of the blue, a stranger approached me and said, "Mr. Jeffers, let me lend you a hand." As we made our way inside, another member came up to ask if I needed help. To my delight, several others expressed their pleasure at seeing me again. To borrow a phrase from Glenn, their attention and kindness made me "feel like a million bucks."

I spent about an hour with Zondra in our exercise room. She acquired reports on my leg from the doctor and worked to understand my relative leg strength and mobility issues. We did a few exercises, like a yoga one-legged standing exercise, knee bends, and such. She also suggested I come in here and lift to improve my overall core strength. The facilities in the Club are good, with a Universal Gym, exercise bikes, and free weights.

I worked on our discussion and then walked out to the practice green to putt. There, I was literally inundated with members offering positive well-wishes and encouragement. I put the cane down and attempted some putts. It was slow at first, but I could shuffle around enough to get some practice.

I strode toward the practice range to say hi to Jeff, my instructor. It involved a challenging walk down to the practice area. I elected to leave him alone. I then hobbled to the loop shed to say hi to Tim and the boys. Again, the guys there could not have been nicer. One of them mentioned that several members have asked when you will be available for private lessons. I caught Tim as I was walking out. He took my clubs and gave them to the club storage attendant. I then commented on how well I had been treated out there. He then said something I thought that struck me. He said, "You are like a God around here. Club members see you like family. ". I have not thought about Club members as a type of family or being people who cared about me. I obviously need to re-think that.

On the drive home, I reflected on that with renewed energy and enthusiasm. The members of the Club were a great inspiration. There was a time when I thought golf was something in my past. I have no idea if I can get back to where I was before the shooting. But I am determined to try. The Club will be at my back, pushing me forward.

I spent the next couple of weeks doing exercises nearly non-stop. By the end, I can now slowly limp around the community trail. I am getting it so I can putt and chip without frequent rest stops.

I was outside putting in the backyard when Glenn yelled at me to come in and check this out. His voice had a rare sound of urgency, so I hurried in, almost stumbling. It was a news report on Rory. The report said he was initially charged with 2nd-degree murder but pleaded it down to attempted murder and involuntary manslaughter. I asked Glenn how much time he thinks he will serve. Glenn thought he would probably receive a 10-year prison sentence but will probably serve 5.

I called Jen later to catch her up on the news surrounding Rory. We had a polite conversation, nothing heavy. I told her about my conviction toward my rehab and about the positive results I am seeing. She talked about how she is acclimating herself to the business. She mentioned she had put Grams' house up for sale. I told her my SATs were next week, but we could get together for coffee after that. She said she would like that.

SAT preparations were a grind. Glenn signed me up for a prep course, and I spent evenings learning vocabulary and memorizing math formulas and problems. The math section came easily, but the verbal was a bear.

The exam itself was on a Saturday in the school cafeteria. As expected, the math section came easily while the verbal section was a struggle. After 8 hours of testing, I have had it.

A couple of weeks later, the results envelope arrived. I was almost too anxious to open the envelope. I ripped it open, then subtly peaked at the scores.   460 verbal, 740 math for a 1200 total. I called Jen, explaining my utter disappointment that she beat me by 20 points. She laughed. I then asked her if she would meet for coffee on Wednesday. She initially hedged somewhat that felt like a 'No' was on the horizon. Then she said, "OK., I will see you at ten at the usual spot." At that moment, I felt as though some of the shroud of gray hovering over me was starting to give way to a bluer sky.

My next call following the call to Jen went out to the Georgia Tech golf coach. Most college golf programs that had shown interest backed off once they learned of my troubled past and challenging rehab. Georgia Tech and Augusta University were two that had not wavered in their support since the shooting. I am learning about Georgia Tech primarily due to its engineering program, which is ranked among the best in the nation. They have also had several quality golfers go through their program: Matt Kuchar, Stewart Cink, Larry Mize, and Cameron Tringale.

I sent over my transcripts to the Georgia Tech coach, along with my SAT scores. He invited me over for a quick visit the very next day. I accepted and met him at his office in the athletic department. He was very personable, showing me around the athletic facilities. We then walked to the engineering department even though my walking was still impaired. While there, I couldn't help but see a couple of monuments dedicated to Bobby Jones. "Did you know Bobby attended Georgia Tech back around 1920?" the Tech coach mentioned. He added, "Our golf teams play at East Lake and the Golf Club of Georgia. That is in Alpharetta, which is close to you. I mentioned that I still have agonizing memories of East Lake, although I could see why it is a highly respected course.

After the coach's tour wound down, he sat me down in his office and said, "I think you are an amazing golf talent, a generational talent. We want that talent at Georgia Tech. I understand you have a lot of work to do to get your body back into golf shape. You can and will do that. I am prepared to offer you a one-year scholarship starting in January. I am prepared to extend that to you, provided you can regain the form you exhibited at your District Championship. What do you think? "I responded with, "That sounds awesome. I am here because Georgia Tech was loyal to me while others were not. If I accept this, I will not disappoint you." The coach responded with a lot of Southern charm: "I believe that too, son ." I then asked if I could have a little time to review his offer, and he told me to take as much time as I needed.

I drove home with my head in the clouds. Receiving an athletic scholarship was something I never thought could be in the cards for me. My overriding thought. I cannot wait to tell Jen.

I walked into our coffee shop the following day feeling positive and excited. I sat down in my chair across from Jen and, in an elated tone, said, "Guess what? I received a scholarship offer from Georgia Tech." Congratulations! That is excellent news," she replied. Usually, I would melt over her adulation. However, this time, her tone was more polite than excited. My exuberance quickly gave way to agony as I realized my old Jen was not back.

We exchanged small talk over the next half an hour or so. I dropped a couple of hints about her attending Tech. I suggested she could study business and still stay active with the company. She countered that she was a Vandy girl by birth, and that was where she would go if the opportunity allowed. She suggested she is too busy for school at this point.

We got to the point where we exhausted all the outstanding topics. We discussed my rehab, my golf game, and Glenn's progress. I asked her about her house sale and her new digs. I really wanted to ask her if she was seeing anyone. But the truth be known, I was scared shitless about what she might say. Instead, I asked her if she would like to come over for a BBQ sometime. There was a brief moment of silence, like she needed to consider the request carefully. I then added that I knew Glenn would love to see you. She said "Sure" in one of those tones that did not communicate a lot of certainty. We walked out the door to our respective cars. Then she said, "Let's stay in touch."

As I walked away, I thought to myself, "Fuck". Jen is slipping away, and there is nothing I can do.

It was a long drive home. In fact, I didn't want to go home, so I went out to the Club to putt a little. After a bit of practice, I got a cart and drove out to the bench of hole 3. I always liked the view from there. Jen and I used to go there after dark and make out. I sat there and reflected on the status of my life. At this moment, golf seems like it is all I have. Re-establishing my golf game has to be a priority. At the same time, there is a hole in my heart that is currently consuming me. I hope golf can fill it. This is hell.

Later in the afternoon, after spending the bulk of the day sulking and feeling sorry for myself, I decided to return home, hoping Glenn might provide some solace. I have an indescribable void in my life, and looking to Glenn for solace has to be considered a sheer act of desperation.

When I walked in, Glenn was where you usually find him sitting in his chair during happy hour and beyond, reading a book with a glass of Scotch. I said, "Hey, Glenn, do you have a minute?". Glenn put down his book and asked, "What's on your mind, son?". I explained to him that since Isla's death, Jen has been heavily involved in her family's business and does not seem to care about me anymore. "Any thoughts, ideas, infamous words of wisdom?" I asked.

Glenn then took his reading glasses off and said. "I lived with a woman for 20 years and never figured out the species. With that as a disclaimer, let me tell you this", as he sat back in his chair. "People change. What they need at one stage in your life may not be the same at another stage." He then asked me, "Have you considered that maybe she feels obligated to put all her focus on trying to sustain her family's legacy?" Glenn's comment suddenly hit a chord that made perfect sense. I responded, "Glenn, you may be on to something." Glenn added, "Maybe she needs a friend more than she needs a boyfriend right now. Love means that sometimes you do what is best for that person.   Figure out how to be her friend for now and see where things go." He then placed his reading glasses back on and stuck his nose back in his book.

I went out on the patio. The fan was spinning, which kept things cool. That was an excellent place to reflect. I know I give Glenn shit about his curt advice that is rarely on target. However, he hit a home run this time.   I am still hurting now, but not nearly as bad thanks to Glenn. I have important things to work on. My rehab, my golf. Hopefully, they are enough to change my focus for now.

Glenn and I have a breakthrough

It has been about four months since the accident. My lazy summer days are spent mainly at the golf course. I have backed off the rehab a bit, taking sessions only once every other week. Overall, my leg is getting stronger. It is far from where it was, but I can put enough weight on it to swing normally. My biggest issue is leg strength. I can play a few holes with a cart, but certain shots are challenging. My body turn during the backswing, a vital swing component, is also limited by the injury to that quad muscle.

I restarted lessons with Jeff. My swing is off, nothing gross– but I need to determine if the best strategy is to wait until my body is correct or make some mods to allow me to work around the afflictions. I probably need to involve my Tech coach for his advice. Coach, as I call him, phones me about once a week to check on my progress. I appreciate that. He seems like a good guy who genuinely cares about me.

After today's lesson, I texted Glenn and asked him to join me for a few holes. I was expecting one of his curt comments, e.g., 'Not Today.' He has hesitated to test his injury, which seems to have recovered well. He also has cut back his work day somewhat. He used to work continuously but may be more interested in trying to smell some roses. "See you at 3," he said. I was surprised.

After hitting a few practice balls, we both played a few holes. I'm still relying on a golf cart for now. Glenn played better than he had certainly ever expected. As we walked off the number

3 green, Glenn said, let's go over to the bench and sit awhile. We sat down, and Glenn smiled and said, "Thanks, Jack, for getting me out here and off my ass. I forget how enjoyable this is." I nodded in response to Glenn's remarks. I explained to him that I have been doing a lot of reflecting lately. Glenn smiled, knowing exactly what I meant. I told Glenn I could do my best thinking out on the course. "The beauty of the golf course, the sound of birds, the smell of freshly cut grass. It brings me peace.:"

"You know that I proposed to Abigail right here." Glenn pointed to where the bench was located at the time. It was higher up and looked out over the grounds. "This was an extraordinary place for us," Glenn responded, sounding a bit nostalgic. "Was she a golfer?" I asked. "Yes, kind of. I think she played mostly because she enjoyed being out here with me. Whenever we traveled, we would stop at golf courses, not to play but to enjoy the ambiance. Hanging out at golf courses was just our thing."

"Glenn, I do get it," I replied. "For me, I think about all the golfers who have played here and wonder what effect the game has had upon their lives. For some people, their motivation may be the social element. Others may play here to get exercise. Still, others may come here to test their manhood with a driver. You came here to share a special time with the woman you love. I came here to perfect my golf skills. A lot of people. A lot of circumstances. One special game."

"As an FYI, hanging out at golf courses was Jen and my thing, too," I added.

Glenn adds, "As much as I love this place, peace for me is a bit of a work-in-process. God and I are still in some heated negotiations." he smiles subtly. "I have lost family members. But I have gained you. One thing I have learned as a lawyer is that in negotiations, you rarely get everything you want. In the legal world, getting much of what you want is considered good negotiation." He put his arm on my shoulder and said, "Let's go get some dinner." We returned to the golf cart, chatted, and headed to the clubhouse. We talked about my rehab, upcoming college next year, and Jen. As I reflected on the previous few hours, Ithought to myself. "This was a great day,".

Chapter 6

College and the Search for Family

Since our coffee in June, I have had several phone conversations with Jen. There does not appear to be that love connection I have known, which I find almost unbearable. I am listening to Glenn and trying to keep my emotions under wraps. My focus is on her friendship, and I am slowly getting more and more comfortable with that. Having her available to talk to is worlds ahead of the silence thing. It's not ideal, but OK.

She called me last night. That was a first. She had something important on her mind that she really wanted to discuss. She said, "With Grams gone, I have found myself thinking a lot about my parents. If you recall, they died before I knew them. Grams spoke often of the greater Laird family. They were a strong, close family that worked together. They would commonly have family events and reunions. The family unit and lineage were known and clear to all. However, I have recently realized that I knew almost nothing about the McGregors, my mom's family."

Then she said, "I reflected on you for a moment and realized you don't know about your parents or greater family. Are you ever curious? " I responded, "Of course I am. For a long time, I harbored a lot of anger toward my parents who abandoned me. I might have even used that anger to justify the trouble I got into growing up. As I have matured–if that is even an accurate statement–I have softened some of those hard edges. All people have stuff. I get how having a baby in the middle of a difficult situation would be hard. But to answer your question, yes, I have been thinking about it more."

I told Jen that I considered trying to find my mom by researching birth records. Glenn told me that Georgia law essentially does not allow me to see my birth mother unless she wants to be found.

Jen then told me about something she saw on TV called 23andMe. She said you submit your saliva to this company, and then they do DNA sampling. They use that information to tell you about your country or origin. They can also show–and even link–you to people you are related to who have also taken the test. "We should do this?" she said.

I talked to Glenn about this, feeling like it was a matter of respect to tell him what we discussed. I informed him, "Glenn, you have been more of a father to me than anyone else in my life. Regardless of what I find, nothing will change that or the gratitude I feel for all you have done for me ". Glenn reached across the table and grabbed my hand. He said, "Thank you, son. Take the test".

Jen ordered the kits, and we met at the coffee shop. She read the instructions and led us through the process. She said it would take a few weeks. "I will submit these. Shall we open our results together?" she said. I nodded. She had to run to a meeting but will let me know when the results come back.

Those three weeks could not come fast enough. In the meantime, I occupied myself, sticking with my daily strength training regimen and working on my game. Having a daily regimen keeps my mind occupied and focused on the positives. After a long rehab, I am finally making progress. I can walk nine holes now without much pain. I elected to stick with my old swing, expecting the body to return to normal eventually. The Tech coach, Jeff, and even Glenn agreed. Looking back, that was a smart move. I am getting closer. I should be able to execute once I can bring a full turn without pain. I had a 37 yesterday, which felt comfortable.

Even though I am playing better, I plan to skip the Club Junior championship this year and will instead target the Club Championship in September. The Tech coach suggested that I work in a couple of AJGA (American Junior Golf Association) tournaments before entering the college routine. In the meantime, I will listen to my instructors and focus on building and rehabbing my body.

Three weeks passed quickly. As it approached, I watched the phone, waiting for Jen's call about the 23andme results. Finally, her call came. Jen said with some excitement in her voice, "I got the results and cannot wait to share what they say. Let's meet at 10 am at our coffee shop." I said, "I will see you there." I spent the entire evening wondering what to find…or if I was ready to learn about my past. It was almost more than I could process. However, what I did know was that I was excited to spend more time with Jen.

I walked into the coffee shop, and Jen was smiling with enthusiasm, almost bouncing in her chair.

She eagerly opened her envelope and, to no surprise, barely waited until I sat down. It established that her heritage was predominantly Scottish. DNA relatives show people related to you who may have also used the service. For the DNA match, there were quite a few entries. "There is less here than I have seen with others." she said. She has a couple of 2nd cousins on the McGregor (mother) side. Both appear to be in the area. Her grandmother on her mom's side is Gillespie. There were a couple of cousins listed there as well. There were a few distant Laird relatives, Tobias and Gramme, whose relation was unknown. I doubt we found anything one would call groundbreaking in her report, although it does provide her with numerous avenues to pursue so that she could begin filling in holes.

Jen then opened my envelope. It also showed my heritage as predominantly Scottish—an interesting coincidence. A block of other backgrounds ranged from English to East European. For my DNA relatives, mine included two entries: Elspeth Laird, daughter of Graeme and Roslin Laird. It also had an Ashleigh Dickenson, relation unknown.

As we viewed my results, we stared at one another in amazement. An obvious question was on our minds, although neither of us could get the nerve to speak it. Could Jen and I be related? Jen finally said it. "I wonder how our common relative, Gramme Laird, is related to each of us? Could we possibly be related? I am also puzzled, " she said, "If Gramme Laird is a common relative, why isn't Elspeth on my list, and why isn't Tobias on your list?"

The Search Begins

Jen and I settled on having coffee meet-ups on Wednesday every other week. She seems exceptionally determined to solve this ancestral conundrum. Much more than me I think, My overriding motivation is to spend time and share an experience with Jen. I am eagerly on board if exploring our respective ancestry is the vehicle.

I do want to know where I came from and learn who my parents are and why they gave me up for adoption. I am also very intrigued with unraveling the question surrounding the Gramme Laird and how that may link Jen and myself. At the same time, I am afraid of where this journey takes us. Am I going to find out that I came from a line of losers and druggies or that I was the lovechild of some skanky prostitute who needed to turn tricks to finance her drug habit? Another concern. Will I discover that Jen and I are related in a way that undermines our future?

I was chatting with Glenn about all of this. He thought, despite the concerns, it was a worthwhile pursuit. Glenn said, "Knowing is always better than not knowing. People can deal with what they know. They can be haunted by what they don't." Glenn always seemed armed with quotes and words of wisdom to fit nearly any situation. I asked him once how he came up with all this stuff. He said Pop Andrews, as we called him, had sayings for everything. "Over time, you hear the same ones over and over so often that they start to become part of your lexicon. " smiling as he quipped. He had one more to share. "It is better to embrace your adventure than fear the destination. This is how I would approach this family search. Embrace the adventure."

Jen and I mapped out a game plan. She was a planner and highly organized in most things she did. Jen will makes and works the list in order while I typically find the most enjoyable item and start there. She planned to delve back through her lineage and try to solve her connection to Tobias and Gramme. That would entail interviews with the few remaining family members and looking through Gram's letters and photos. Hopefully, that could lead us to Elspeth. I would start looking through the Internet to find Ashleigh Dickenson.

Jen had identified three possible sources of older family information. One of those was Grams' sister; the other two needed to be located. Jen reached out to her Aunt, although they had a very contentious encounter at Gram's house, which Jen all but threw her Aunt out of the Grams' house. Jen approached her Aunt with reluctance. Jen asked her if she knew Tobias or Gramme Laird. She replied with an emphatic "No." While Jen and I discussed the situation, we wondered if her Aunt would have disclosed information, even if known. Jen explained that her Aunt was a family outsider—maybe even an outcast. Her odds of being plugged into the family network and knowing relatives were probably low.

In my search for Ashleigh Dickenson, I told Jen that I was looking for someone between 12 and 30 years old who lives in the greater Georgia area. I found a website that locates people. They found 137 potential candidates. I have started going through names one at a time. Jen then asked me, "How are you approaching these people?" I told her, "I said to them that I was abandoned at birth in the Atlanta area and was looking for my natural parents. My 23andMe report says that I am a 20-year-old relative of Ashleigh Dickenson, and I wondered if that person could be you. " Jen offered a couple of suggestions to my pitch but liked my spiel overall.

We met up a week later. I have yet to make progress to report, although I have gone through nearly 100 of the 137 names. I told her I had gotten a lot of hang-ups, but most were polite and said they were not the person I was looking for. They wished me the best of luck in my search. I got a couple of people who might entertain the notion of being related to someone they didn't know. They then asked, how would we know if we are related? If you submitted a 23andMe, then we would have a vital clue. They generally responded that they were unsure if they wanted to know that badly.

I then explained to Jen how this whole thing was a real shot in the dark. I am not sure how I am related to Ashleigh. She may not care about family relations. She could live out of the area. She could also be outside the age parameters we are searching for. I told her I would keep working and finish with the remaining names, but we needed more clues.

Jen showed a lot of perseverance and sticktoitiveness. She assures me we will turn something up if we stay with the plan. At the same time, Jen expressed some frustration in her research. She had concluded that Tobias was probably a relative related to a great-grandfather. She said, "I know the information is out there. We just have to keep digging to find it." Despite the setbacks, I was impressed with Jen's determination. She does not give up easily. That is good quality.

I explained to her that I would need to miss our next meeting. I told her I had Club Championships, my first competitive tournament since the accident. She mentioned that she would like to get out and see it. But unfortunately, work issues have her very bogged down. My initial reaction was that the old Jen would have attended my tournament. After a brief moment of reflection, I realized that our relationship is different and I should not judge her based on previous behaviors. It sucks for sure, but it is the way it is.

Club Championship

There are a lot of question marks heading into this 2-day tournament. Those questions have me concerned yet excited. My past month has consisted of grueling daily workouts in the weight room and extended training and practice on the course. Logic would suggest I should feel ready, given the extent of my preparation, but you only know where your game is once it is tested in the heat of competition.

I'm ready. Let's go.

As I walked up to the 1st tee, I was surprised by the number of people who came to watch my round. There were a couple of articles published that described my fight back. I imagine the buzz surrounds people's curiosity. For a moment, I wondered if maybe my playing partners had large families. However, that question was quickly answered as the crowd, who were generally chatting, became eerily quiet during my tee shot. With all the chatter, I stepped away from the shot to gather myself. I looked around the gallery of maybe 50 or so to see if Jen was there. I did not find her there, although I did see my Tech coach.

My opening tee shot reflected the distraction. It went into the pines on the right. "Shit," I said as the ball sliced to the right. The ball was so far right I feared a lost ball, forcing me to hit a provisional tee shot. You get 3 minutes to find your ball, which was not long enough, apparently. I ended up taking the lost ball penalty and playing the provisional. A double bogey on the first hole was not what I was looking for after the weeks of anticipation.

I righted the ship somewhat on the next hole with a par. The 3rd hole needed a great chip to save par. Likewise, 4th and 5th holes required quality saves after I put myself in trouble off the tee. That pretty much described the round. It was a grind from the opening shot. Still, a 75 was a decent score, given my struggles. I am 7 strokes behind the leader and probably out of contention. My leg is very sore. I did not take a cart, which I had considered. I suggest reconsidering that for tomorrow. For now, I am headed to Glenn's hot tub.

I was talking with my friend Tim after the round. He came over to the house for some BBQ. We sat on the porch, waiting for the ribs to cool. I was explaining how I let thoughts of Jen creep into my consciousness. I hate to say, but she disrupted my round.

Tim offered that this type of thing comes up often with golfers. He suggested, "When your mind wanders to things unrelated to golf, you are not staying present. Your mind needs to focus on things happening on the golf course. When you sense your mind wandering, tell yourself to Stop!, then mentally turn the page to matters on the course. "

I started the 2nd day with a new attitude and a golf cart. My game responded appropriately. I was sharp and on target throughout the front nine, shooting an impressive 31. My hot golf continued during the first part of the 2nd nine. I started par, birdie, birdie, eagle. Even though I was riding in the cart, my leg still felt the strain of play. I bogeyed that last three holes to finish as 34. That gave me a 65 for the day. Good for 2nd. I was initially bummed when I found out I was only one stroke away from 1st. But Tim approached me and got my head right as he routinely does. You dug yourself a big hole on day one but came back and put up a significant number today. "Look at this as a springboard to a complete recovery," Tim responded. I pondered his comment for a moment, then accepted his wisdom.

I got a call that evening from the Tech coach. He has been closely monitoring my progress. He always makes me feel like he is more concerned with Jack Jeffers, the person than he is with Jack Jeffers, the golfer. I greatly respect that, which is why I chose Georgia Tech. However, this call felt different to me. He was there for my ho-hum 1st day round, where he was less than impressed. I talked to him about my vital 2nd day round and 2nd place finish overall. He was encouraged by my improvement.

I asked him since I have you on the phone, "you mentioned that my scholarship is conditional on my game returning to the pre-injury form. How do we measure that, and when will I know I can register for the Spring semester?" He said that he prides himself in being straight with his athletes. At the same time, he said he does not want to bring any golfer into his program who cannot succeed. He said he is encouraged by the trend of my recovery and was committed to formalizing their agreement by December 1.

After that somewhat awkward conversation with the Tech coach, Glenn and I debriefed the call. Glenn reminds me that I technically do not have any agreement with Tech. He asserts that he has built a career in reading people and situations. I can believe that. He said that I need to remember that as cordial as the Tech coach appears, he also has a job to do, which is to field a championship team. He said, "This may sound cold, but remember, you are only a tool at his disposal. He would not hedge by waiting until December 1 if he had total faith in you. He would have laid a contract in front of you to sign today."

Glenn gave me a lot of reasons for pause. I sat there for several minutes in dead silence, reflecting on his comments. He then proposed another option he wanted me to seriously consider. He said, "Jack, you don't need to feel like you are being held hostage by Georgia Tech. I can afford to send you to any school you want to attend. " I responded, "That is awfully generous of you, Glenn. You have already done so much for me. I don't know…" I said. "Just file it!" Glenn said in closing.

Wow, I thought to myself. That Tech coach had me feeling like a hostage; now, thanks to Glenn's generosity, I am back in control. Thank you, Glenn. You are too good to me.

I spent the day or so reflecting on my situation. I didn't even go to the golf course.

Following my path

I am feeling shaken by the state of my college golf aspirations. I started this fall expecting my scholarship to be all but a done deal if I could re-establish my game. My naivete was exposed when I discovered my scholarship was anything but certain. Another thing Glenn mentioned was, "Consider that the schedule for a college golf athlete can be demanding. While I know you are not afraid of work, remember that the work may not necessarily conform to your schedule or needs. You also have different people managing your career who have other priorities. They may not even be effective career managers. I am not trying to steer you in any way. I want you to know that you have done a fantastic job of managing your own golf career. Are you sure you want to turn that over to others? You have options."

The Tech Coach wanted me to play in a couple of AJGA events. I have decided to overrule him with a different plan. I am going to play at the US Mid-Amateur Championship in the latter part of October. This tournament features most of the top amateurs in the region. It is also played at the Country Club of Columbus in Columbus, Ga. This is a course I played during last year's golf season, and it seems to fit my game really well. That also gives me time to work on some weaknesses between now and then.

Glenn has a quote that sits well with me: "You are remembered for the rules you break." As I understand it, this was a quote from General McArthur. It does not suggest anything violent or illegal but suggests those who choose non-standard paths will be seen differently and remembered for doing it their way. "Think Bobby Jones," Glenn said. "He was considered the best golfer in the world. Everyone expected him to turn pro, yet he broke the rules and remained an amateur. He lived on his terms such that we are still talking about him 100 years later for his bold choice."

Inspired by Glenn's support, I enrolled at Georgia Tech with a light schedule.

I met Jen for coffee on Wednesday with a lot to catch up on. I told her about my 2nd place finish at the Club Champion. We also discussed how the Georgia Tech coach appeared to waffle on my scholarship. With Glenn's economic support, I am planning to follow my path. I also enrolled at Tech for the fall semester. "What's new with you?" I chuckled.

"Not much," she said, pausing to add more. "Here is a coincidence for you. I also enrolled at Georgia Tech. I am just taking a few night classes in business school. "that's a start. After finishing our discussion on classes and schedules, she asked me how I was coming on the list of names I was calling. I told her I had called them all and left my number where possible. I hope someone in that group has a revelation or finds me in their 23andMe search, but at least I made the effort.

"How is your search coming?" I asked. Jen said she had exhausted her family sources and was planning a new path. "I am going to see if I can find a US marriage certificate for Gramme and Roslin Laird." I smiled and nodded. We chatted longer and then agreed to reconvene in a few weeks.

A couple of weeks later. I received an unexpected call from the Tech coach. He was asking me how the AJGA tournament went over the weekend. Of course, I didn't play in that tournament as we had discussed. I am sitting here in fear, wondering exactly how to describe my defiance. I am also debating exactly how much I want to communicate.

The conversation was tense, as I anticipated. The Georgia Tech coach wanted to know why I didn't play in the tournament. He said he couldn't sign off on my scholarship until I proved myself in more tournaments. I told him we had talked about all that, but then I told him something bold. I said, " I understand your expectations. However, I am responsible for my golf career until I am officially on your team. " Feeling like I was on a roll of pure, brutal honesty, I added news he would not likely appreciate. "I am currently attending the Fall Semester at Tech. Based on my direction, I may not need a golf scholarship after all." He then tried to backpedal, ensuring I knew Tech was still committed to me. I thought to myself, yeah, right. I laid the hammer down with this last statement. "If Tech was committed to me, wouldn't I be under scholarship already?" As a matter of courtesy, I finished by telling him to stay in touch. I think he knew what that meant.

Fall Semester at Tech

I started my 1st semester at Tech with only three classes: Introduction to Engineering, Calculus, and Introduction to Computer Programming. When Glenn saw the classes I had scheduled, his first question was, "Those look like pretty difficult classes. Are you sure you can handle all that and have enough in the tank to be fair to your golf game?" I explained that I took some Calculus in high school. I have also done a lot of computer coding over the years. I am expecting those to come easily. The most difficult one so far has been the Introduction to Engineering. I thought I understood Engineering before I enrolled. I even picked up the textbook and thumbed through it, figuring it would help me know what I would study. While I like the class, it has been a challenge so far. Fortunately, I can complete all my coursework two mornings a week.

One evening, I needed to spend time in the computer lab working on a programming assignment. I finished the lab work and walked to the Jeep with one of my classmates. On the walkway close to my path, I spotted what I am sure was Jen. She was walking with a guy. This guy seemed like a real faceman...a very good-looking guy. Shit! I thought to myself. Every part of my being wanted to follow her, but the guy I was walking with was telling me something personal. That would have been shitty of me to dump him like that. Funny. I had never thought of Jen and somebody else. For some reason, it just never tripped my consciousness. Now thinking about it makes me feel like shit. There was only one thought swirling inside my head. "Have I lost her for real this time?". I had also considered confronting her a week after her evening class but later decided against it. I decided to talk to her at the coffee shop on Wednesday next week.

I knew the coffee meet-up would be tense–perhaps contentious–as I walked inside the door. Part of me wonders if I will hear something I do not want to hear. At the same time, I told myself to 'man up' and not appear weak in front of her. I saw her sitting there with her red hair, and then, as always, my heart simply melts when I look at her. I wonder what she thinks when she sees me.

We talked about our ancestry search, and she said she just found a contact who could let her into the LexisNexis system in the Law Library. "LexisNexis is an online service that allows you to search official records. Like business records, deeds, and such. I. You can also search marriage records, although it is not perfect. I will tell you how that all works out." she explained.

We discussed the usual topics like golf, school, and her business. I then got up the nerve to ask her. "Are you seeing someone?" She was initially shocked at the question and said, "What?" forcing me to repeat the question. I asked again, "Are you seeing someone?" She then says, "Why do you ask?" I told her I saw her with some guy at school and needed to ask. She explained that the guy I was referring to was an acquaintance hooking me up to the LexisNexis system. "I think he would like to date me, but I told him I was not emotionally available," Jen explained. "Oh," I said, feeling like a total dickhead.

She came back to me asking if I was dating anyone. I told her, "No. For similar reasons.." I then looked carefully at her expression to see if there was anything I could learn about her feelings. Unfortunately no. Jen was certainly no card player but was very good at keeping a poker face. We closed with a joint agreement that we would tell the other if we were to date. OK, I thought, feeling like things were not out of control, at least for now.

That evening, Glenn asked me how school was progressing. I told him that I was feeling very good about it. I enjoyed the subject matter of the courses I am studying. I said This may sound strange, but I even look forward to attending classes and learning. It is a needed diversion from my golf regimen.

Glenn then countered with another of his sayings, as he often does. He said, "I operate by an adage you might find useful. Love your job and you will never work another day in your life. Maybe that saying applies to school as well. Think about it."

Chapter 7

Jack Proves Game in Amateur Tournaments

We had mapped out a fall-season tournament schedule that would either make or break me. The Tech coach wanted me to slide into college play. Instead, I tried to take control of my career and push myself against the best amateur competition. Jeff and I picked out four tournaments over the next three months that drew regional and International competitions. Jeff thinks I am ready. I have characterized this upcoming stretch of tournaments as 'The Gauntlet'

The Mid-Amateur in Columbus is just two days away. Usually, I feel a lot more together. Nowadays, I have so much going on with school, Jen, and such that golf does not feel like it dominates me anymore. Glenn says that is probably a good thing. "People need balance in their lives," he says. Still, I have been putting the work in. Morning range balls, except for Tuesday / Thursday. Every day, I play a 9-hole practice round. Afterwards, I work on any problem areas. On Saturday, I have a routine lesson with Jeff where he scopes my swing to ensure consistency. We then talked about some areas I am working on, and he may work with me on a few specialty shots. I work on putting and chipping at home.

Now that I am in school I don't have any income coming in. Thankfully, with Glenn's generous graduation gift and his financing of my education, I am OK. I would not be able to do this otherwise. Instead, I would be sucking up to the Tech coach on my knees in an embarrassing display.

Mid-Amateur in Columbus

I talked Tim into driving out and looping for me in Columbus. He is a great asset. The long drive to West Georgia allowed us to get caught up. Tim also had time to ensure my head was right, which seems like an ongoing issue.

We arrived at the Country Club mid-afternoon the day before the tournament. I have played the course several times and felt familiar with the layout. Tim walked the course and took some notes, while I went through my range ball, putting and chipping regimen. After the practice, I felt ready going into tomorrow. At the same time, I was also uneasy knowing that I had not played competitively in a couple of months. This tournament field would also be the stiffest competition I have faced in my young career.

I walked to the tee as the youngest competitor in the tournament. My two playing partners were probably in their 30s. I saw one of them on the driving range. Man, could he bomb the ball? I pulled in on a golf cart. The other players must have thought I was a marshal or an onlooker from the Country Club. Using a golf cart is generally considered taboo. Fortunately, my high school golf coach is well-connected in the GGA (Georgia Golf Association) and got me a 'medical variance' as it is called. Still, I wondered if they thought I might be getting an unfair advantage. I was also among the few golfers there using a caddie. I am sure all of this raised some eyebrows also.

Minor controversies aside, the 1st day of the tournament could not have gone better. Of course, it could have gone better; I could have made all birdies and maybe even some more eagles. But I played as well as I have. I shot a 64, which put me in the lead by 3. My playing partners were outdriving me by 40 yards on some occasions. I just stuck to my game, which is based on consistency and accuracy, not distance. Once I began piling up birdies, there was a lot of complaining about my use of the cart. Tim was a great help in keeping me focused and in my lane despite the distractions.

After the round, Tim and I spent about 10 minutes doing some stretches. Then, we went to the deck area outside the lounge to chill. The guys around me were generally cool. A couple told me a nice round. But there were also the usual dicks. One of the competitors asked me if he could buy me a drink. Full knowing neither of us was 21. I surprised him and said sure, give us a couple of Arnold Palmer's. Another dick told me that I should try walking the course. It is a lot more work.

Let that shit slide." Tim said. "You aren't going to win big tournaments with your mouth." Yet, I still wondered if I had an advantage.

For play on the 2nd day, I elected not to use a golf cart. I know this would be hard on my body, but at the same time, I did not want an asterisk on my scorecard, suggesting my success was attributed to an aid. My playing opponent commented off-hand about my use of the golf cart. "I thought you couldn't walk," he said. "That's just posturing, Jack. Ignore it." Tim said.

On the 2nd day of the tournament, I started out solid. On the front nine, I was 3-under. My challenger played really well and shot a 31 to close within two strokes. He continued his hot play into the 2nd nine. He trailed by one going into the par five 17th hole. If you can place your tee shot, this hole has a very reachable green. The challenger thought he could drive over the hazard with a long tee ball. I put a perfect three-wood just in front of the trap that would require a lay-up. My competitor hit a tremendous drive over the trees that I figured was clear of danger. Instead, it was a little short, falling in some deep grass. I put my approach shot on the front of the green. My opponent tried to do too much with a mid-iron, and his shot came up short in a creek bed. He then tried a miracle shot from a tough lie and hit it out of bounds. I holed out a 30-foot putt from off the green for an eagle. My competitor 3-putted for a triple that all-but-sealed my victory. I added an exclamation point with a birdie on the closing 18th to finish with a 63, winning by eight impressive strokes.

I was on cloud nine as I signed my final scorecard. "We did it, Dude!" I told Tim as I gave him a big hug. "It was you, man. "Tim replied, but I countered that we are a good team. "An amazing team," Tim added, acknowledging that he was a measurable contributor.

We grabbed some dinner, and I replayed many of the significant events during the day. It was perfect to get that monkey off my back from playing with a cart. I am sore, but overall OK. I will be able to walk most courses from now on. Avoiding an overly hilly layout would be necessary.

As we walked out, a competitor who seemed a little older than me walked up and congratulated me. He told me his name, but it did not register with me. He said that he was a golfer from the Georgia Tech golf team. "The fact that you have only been playing for two years is simply incredible," he said. "I just got off the phone with Coach (referring to the golf coach at Tech). He said he wants to offer you a scholarship. It would be great to have you on our team. We could be a national contender with a guy like you on the roster.

"Let me tell you a story," I replied as I eased back in my chair. I went on to explain how, six months ago, I was shot in the upper leg while lying in a hospital with what many thought could be a career-ending injury. At the very least, I was in for a long, difficult rehab—most college recruiters who seemed highly interested in me all but disappeared. The Tech Coach stayed with me, which I appreciated. However, when it came down to it, he was not nearly as committed as he let on. He was just a nicer version of those who kicked me toward the curb, waiting for me to prove myself once again.

I explained to the golfer that I am currently enrolled at Tech in engineering. I feel like Team Jeffers is managing my game just fine the way it is. I then explained that the coach did not want me to play in this tournament but was pushing me toward the local AJGA event at Brookhaven instead. "Brother! Your golf swing is so fucking smooth. What was our coach thinking?" he responded while shaking his head. I got my point across that his coach misplayed my recruitment.

Jones Cup Invitation at Sea Island

I spoke to my high school golf coach, who congratulated me on an incredibly impressive win. I thanked him for getting me a golf cart variance and explained how I ended up forgoing the cart the 2nd day to make sure people saw my win as legitimate. He understood. I mentioned there was one additional favor I needed to ask. I explained that I wanted to play in the Jones Cup Invitation in November and wondered if he had connections to get me in. The coach said he would see what he could do.

A few days later, he called me back, saying he could pull some strings to get me in. "Their entry is based on World Amateur Golf Rankings, which you do not qualify for yet. I told them about your eight-stroke victory at the Mid-Amateur, and they agreed to let you in due to a recent cancellation." "I owe you," I exclaimed. He said, "Please remember me when you are rich and famous." I just chuckled.

I showed up at Sea Island as a literal nobody in a sea of the world's top amateurs. On the range, I was amazed at how many foreign players were on the field. Again, Tim joined me with his typical control of my psyche. He said, "Nobody knows Jack Jeffers or expects anything from him. Just do your thing. Just stay in your lane, as we always discuss. There aren't any expectations. Let's see what happens."

Sea Island has three championship golf courses. This year's Cup was played at the Seaside Course, the most wide-open of the three but also the most susceptible to the weather. Weather was going to be very influential in my success. Big bombers are going to score well with these wide-open fairways. My game is about consistency and accuracy.

By the time I had teed off, conditions were perfect–for my competitors. No wind. My playing partners were bombers and were consistently 30-40 past me off the tee. Sometimes longer. With all the weightlifting during my rehab, I think I did add to my swing speed. Tim thinks I might be 10 yards farther. Still, Tim reminds me to ignore that. "Stay in your lane. Stay in your lane. "he said. I did. This was easily the most demanding course I have ever played. There were a lot of hidden dangers. Fortunately, Tim had a solid walk-through and was steering me clear.

After the first nine, I was one under.   I had yet to learn how that stood, although my one partner carded a 3-under. On the 2nd nine, I recorded seven straight pars. I was playing well, but it was a day when 10-15-foot putts wouldn't drop. I holed out a brutal 20-foot downhiller on 17 for a birdie. That hole is famous I found out later. They called it the Himalayas and it claims a lot of victims. I then nearly jarred my approach for a tap-in birdie on 18; I finished with a 3-under 67 that put me in 12th place, three strokes behind the leaders on a crowded leaderboard.

Day 2 was the total opposite. While Day 1 was perfectly calm, Day 2 was windy with 15-20 mile per hour winds. There were also multiple storms expected to move through.   The bombers playing short irons into the green yesterday saw the winds owning those shots today. They were hitting long irons and even hybrids today.   My low-piercing shots gave me a distinct advantage.   It's hard to know if that is enough.

The front nine started well. The wind was significant, but I could keep the ball straight with my low-piercing stingers. My putting challenges that haunted me during yesterday's round have disappeared. My front nine ended at a super four under. On the back, I took a bogie on the tough number 13, then eagled 15, followed up with birdies on 16 and 18 for an impressive 64, given the conditions.

I was the current leader, but five other groups were still on the course. Tim and I decided to wait by the 18th green. We watched anxiously as the remaining players came in. The first four groups showed that the weather was a serious factor in their rounds. Of those, only one scored in the 60s. One player in the last group was one stroke ahead of me going into the 18th hole. That player hit his approach into the trap and then played solidly out of the sand. He just needed to hole out a 6-foot putt to win. A strange thing happened as the player walked from the trap to the green. A storm came through with winds approaching 30mph. As the player walked up to mark his ball, his at-rest ball started to move and ended up rolling down the hill, off the green, and down onto the fairway. He could have replaced the ball in a good position had he previously marked the ball. Shaken by his bad luck, his pitch back up the hill was short, and he could not sink the long putt. He finished with a double-bogey 6 to lose to me by one stroke.

That was a significant win for me and will surely put me on the map.

Dixie Amateur Championship and the Timuquana Cup

Following the significant victory at the Jones Cup, receiving invitations to prominent tournaments became a breeze. Florida's amateur tournaments are popular in December and other winter months, but the name Jack Jeffers started to gain traction, and organizers wanted a piece.

Even club manufacturers were also starting to follow me. When I got home, there was a pile of clubs, clothing, and swag. As an amateur, you can't take money or other monetary remuneration. You can, however, receive merchandise with the hope that you will ultimately endorse their products on the pro tour.

The Dixie Amateur and the Timuquana Cup had a strong international field. They both ended much like the Jones Cup, with me coming from behind to win with impressive 2nd day performances.

Following my string of wins, I am now ranked number 3 in the World Amateur Ranking. I have to pinch myself each time I think about it. I have never liked notoriety. I know Glenn doesn't like it. Unfortunately, it has been thrust upon us. The garage is systematically filling up with paraphernalia coming to the house almost daily. Glenn says, "Beware of strangers bearing gifts." He explains that their motives are only sometimes obvious or honorable. College recruiters are still pursuing me, trying to see if I will break ranks as an independent. More and more new articles surface. This one was my favorite. "The Next Tiger?" Come on. Let's get real here.

My next big test will be the George L Coleman Invitational, which will be held in late April. It is a 54-hole event played at the prestigious Augusta Country Club, only a few miles from Augusta National. It has a rich history of hosting the world's top amateurs. Past winners include Hal Sutton, David Duval, Stewart Cink, and Matt Kuchar.

I have some concerns about playing three days in a row. Also, this course is very hilly and will test my conditioning and leg strength. They will not allow golf carts in this tournament. In response, I plan to take a few months off to focus on rehab and get caught up with school work and life.

Glenn frequently reminds me of the importance of work-life balance. I always wonder if that was because he was an 'all-work' guy in his younger years. Golf is still fun, but it could transition into something less desirable. A little time off away from the grind should allow me to absorb the enormity of my successes and recharge the batteries more importantly.

Chapter 8

Jen's New Boyfriend

A month ago, Jen and I had one of our everyday conversations where one of us just called the other and chatted. This time, I called her, wanting to tell her about my win at the Timuquana Cup. I could sense that she was pensive and had something bothering her. Finally, she came clean with me. She said, "Remember when we agreed to tell the other if we were seeing somebody? Well, I need to tell you…that I am seeing somebody. He is a guy from work and is wonderful. I will tell you more later. I hope you are OK. Bye." The conversation closed about as quickly as it started.

For a few days, I was aching inside. It was not necessarily because Jen was seeing someone, but it was her cavalier–I don't give a shit–attitude toward me that hurt me most. Tim thought I needed to invite some fresh females into my life. He is probably right. Still, my plate is pretty full.

I had just finished midterms and was sitting home enjoying some quiet. I felt a tremendous relief to be done with schoolwork for a while. Glenn had dozed off, and I got to thinking about Jen. I decided to call her. Whenever I call, Jen always responds the same way. It is so familiar that I would recognize it anywhere. "Hi Jack, How are you?" she says with this southern charm. This time, however, she went totally off the rails. Without even a hi, she says, "Jack, why are you bothering me at this hour. Don't you know I have my own life...which does not include you. Goodnight, "and she hangs up. I sat back in my chair, feeling shocked. It was almost like I was hearing from someone I did not know.

Over the next few days, that call had me pretty depressed. I realized that I just needed to leave Jen alone for a while. I knew that wasn't going to be easy. I even considered confronting her after work or at school. I realized my pride was above all that, and I just needed to chill.

That night, I was watching a little TV and getting ready to dive into study when the phone rang. I walked in to answer, and it was Jen. She sounded scared and frantic. She cries out, "Jack, please come get me?" She immediately hung up, and I then sprung up, grabbed my keys, and hopped in the Jeep. I sped to her place, ignoring nearly every traffic law in the process; I just prayed I wouldn't get stopped by the police for speeding or worse. It just occurred to me that she was back in Gram's mansion, which I thought was strange.

When I pulled up across the street from her house, I could see somebody toward the back of the house looking inside a window. I immediately turned off my headlights, exited the car, and stealthily crept up quietly without drawing attention. As I got closer, the someone I saw was an older lady. I then realized this was Jen's Aunt, who had moved in with her after Gram's death. I remember her from the funeral. She appeared to be taking a video. Once she saw me, she ran off. I went to the window where the Aunt was standing and saw Jen inside in what seemed like a disparate rage, talking to some guy I assumed was her boyfriend. I climbed through a neighboring window and immediately grabbed Jen, standing behind her and this guy. "Jen and I are leaving," I exclaimed. Her much bigger boyfriend rushes at me to retake control, then shouts with his finger pointed in my face, "You are not taking her anywhere." With a violent shove, I go flying across the floor, and he then comes at me with a wine bottle as if he is going to hit me with it. I then jump up and tackle him in his midsection, and he falls, hitting his head against the dining room table. He lays there motionless momentarily, then rises wobbly to his feet. I grab Jen, and we take off out the front door.

On the drive home, Jen is anxious and talking gibberish almost non-stop. I tried but could not discern what she was saying. When I brought her into the house, Glenn was waiting. He said once he saw her, "She is on something." having dealt with strung-out clients in his past. I thought that also. He called 911. The ambulance took her to the hospital.

Glenn and I drove to the hospital and waited in the waiting room for what seemed like an eternity. Finally, the doctor came in and told us that they found a high concentration of amphetamines in her system. He thought she would be OK but that I should expect her to be groggy for a while as she works past the heavy sedation.

I sent Glenn home and waited by her bed. After a long night, she finally woke up the following day. Once she realized I was there, she squeezed my hand and smiled gently. I sat there with her in virtual silence for over an hour. The doctor came in and talked to her, explaining what they found. They preferred to keep her there for a day or two to remain under observation, but she was free to go whenever she was up to it.

We had lunch in her room while discussing casual things like school, golf, business, etc. She then asked me if I could give her privacy while she made calls. I left the room and sat in the waiting room for about an hour before she appeared with her things, ready to leave. She said she wanted to go to my place when we got in the car. She anxiously tried to tell me what was happening, but for some reason, she wanted Glenn there also.

We walk into the house, and Glenn is cooking up some dinner. He comes over, helps Jen to the couch, and then asks her, "How are you doing?". She responds, "It has been a rough 24 hours," and then goes into a lengthy discussion on what happened.

Jen starts out saying "We hired a new CFO (Chief Financial Officer) at the company several months ago. He started teaching me about finance and many of the business's inner workings. I became attracted to his business acumen that and started seeing him socially, all against my better judgment. He persevered in pursuing a relationship, which felt a little off to me. Then, I began to not feel like myself. Duke, the boyfriend, argued that I was probably stressed with the business. Still, I was experiencing these panic attacks, as I will call them.

Jen then explains, "Last night, I was feeling nauseous and fixed myself a drink of straight vodka to see if that would help. It didn't. I started frantically looking around the cabinets where Grams used to keep some Pepto Bismol, and I came across some pills. I confronted Duke angrily and shouted, "Are you giving me this shit!" I then ran into the bathroom and called you. Everything after that was a fog."

Jen explained that when she asked me for privacy this afternoon, she called the CEO and removed Duke immediately. She then called Duke and told him that if he did not come clean and what he was up to, my next call would be to the police. He did come clean, and what he said was astonishing.

Jen then got this angry expression and explained, "Can you believe Aunt Teresa put him up to this? They planned to get me on video freaking out so that she could declare me mentally incompetent. The court would appoint her conservator as my only blood relative. She would then push me out of the company and get what she considered her birthright, which she believed was stolen from her 30 years earlier.

Glenn interjected, "Do you want me to have these people arrested?". Jen said, "No. But what I would like is if we can get some type of restraining order that keeps Teresa away from me and my company." Glenn said, "Consider that done."

I then asked her if she would like to stay here for a while. She said, "That would be great."

Jen laid low for a few days. She did not say much, and I figured she was trying to get over her traumatic event. To get out of the house, I suggested we go out to the golf course. She didn't play but watched quietly as I practiced. We walked up to our spot off the 3rd tee, where she opened up a little.

She said, "Do you know what the hardest part of this Duke thing is? It is how someone can, almost without conscience, use me and act like they care about me when their motives are evil and dishonest." I wanted to interject but realized I couldn't offer anything to make her feel better. Instead, I nodded as though I understood.

She then changed the subject with a totally different tone and expression. She said, "Before the Duke relationship, I had finished the US search for Gramme and Roslin Laird. Unfortunately, I came up empty on all accounts." She then explained how she got the idea to talk to someone in Gaelic Studies who was familiar with Scottish genealogy. I explained my problem to her, and she suggested we go to Scotland. She gave me some areas to search.

"Jack, why don't we go to Scotland? I could really use a change of scenery," she suggested with heightened exuberance in her voice. "We could check out places where the Lairds might have lived. We could also visit St. Andrews. What do you think?"

Without thinking it through carefully, "I told her, yes, let's go." She said, "I will plan everything."

Chapter 9

Off to Scottland

Jen is the consummate planner.

She arranged the air reservations, our travel itinerary, and our hotel reservations. She even put together some Gaelic phrases for us to use with the locals.

Is e m' ainm Jack [My name is Jack]
Am faigh mi lionn [Can I get a beer]
A bheil sibh eòlach air Elspeth, Gramme neo Roslin Laird [Do you know Elspeth, Gramme or Roslin Laird]

I asked Glenn if he would be able to get along without me. He said jokingly, "I am looking forward to a week of peace," as he smiled.

I have never flown before. In fact, I have bever been in an airport before. Flying is one of those things that is hard to imagine if you have never done it. We have a long flight out of Atlanta and are scheduled to land in Edinburgh on Sunday evening. According to Jen's detailed schedule, we will spend the day in Edinburgh on Monday, sightsee in Inverness on Tuesday, check on small-town Scotland in the southeast (Hawick, Jedburgh, and Selkirk) on Wednesday, and then, who knows, after that. I definitely want to visit the Old Course at St Andrews. That is a must-do. This should all be a fun adventure.

Following a long week of anticipation, we landed in Edinburgh as Jens's plans had laid out. We grabbed a car with this crazy steering wheel on the wrong side. I have seen English movies where they drove that way, but I did not believe that was the thing. Tim always reminds me to stay in my lane on the golf course. I hope I remember what side of that street that is on. We are off to our hotel in Edinburgh. The town is beautiful and much different than Atlanta. There is history and culture everywhere you look. I love the old churches and brick buildings. I bet some of these are hundreds of years old. Jen was in total awe as we passed through some of these historic areas. She reached over and grabbed my hand several times, which was nice.

Jen had warned me about the long odds of finding anything helpful during this trip. However, we both believe that the individuals we seek are in this area, and there should be some documentation of their existence if we only search in the right places. In a way, Jen tries to tamp down expectations; she says that while we may not uncover what we're after on this excursion, at worst, it can be a foundation for a more targeted exploration on a subsequent trip.

We spent most of our first day at the Edinburgh records office and the City Archives. We told the clerk we were searching for three names: Elspeth, Gramme, and Roslin Laird. We are still determining how old they are. Unfortunately, Elspeth and Laird are relatively common names in Scotland. We also have to consider Elspeth was likely married somewhere along the way and could be using her husband's surname. We looked at birth and death records and did not find the right combination of names in Edinburgh. The day was discouraging but as we expected. Putting the search aside, Edinburgh may not have a bad day.

The next day was low key. We drove through the Scottish countryside to the port town of Inverness. I did an excellent job staying in my lane, although I lost focus several times. Jen was generally quiet but then would erupt with "Jack, get in the left lane!." as another car approached. We visited the famous monument Craigh na Dun. We went to an old castle and even stopped at Leakey's Bookshop. We also found the Inverness records office and stepped in. Northwest Scotland is not a common area for the Lairds. Neither of us was expecting to find anybody there and we didn't.

The Lairds were not associated with a Scottish clan but were said to be a commonly adopted name like Jones or Smith. They were much more common in eastern Scotland.

Jen and I are getting along well and had a great day in Inverness exploring the sites, but there are not what I could call feelings of romance right now. I have been extremely hesitant to make any advances or even hold hands, for that matter. Yet, the only option at this hotel we could find was a single double bed. That is going to be weird, I thought to myself. So is the shower. I told Jen I would sleep on the floor. She said, "Don't be ridiculous; I know you are not an attacker." I slept as far right as I possibly could, but it was pretty much butt to butt.

We got up early and drove south into an area that the Scottish Professor at school suggested should be a common area for Lairds. It includes an area approximately 30 x 30 miles south of Edinburgh. During our canvas of the area, we stopped in numerous small towns to check out records offices where we could find them. While those offices yielded no results, these small towns were beautiful and charming. Many have rich histories and buildings dating back hundreds of years or longer. Jen and I share a passion for history and especially love the old churches. When we saw one, we had to stop and check it out.

We were driving through a little town called Galashiels and saw one of those old churches with beautiful stained glass windows. As we had done previously, we stopped, walked around, and observed the artistry and culture. Based on the symbols and inscriptions, this one must be at least several hundred years old. As we were leaving, Jen noticed a plaque on the wall that honored those who fought in WWII. Jen said, "Hey, Jack, check this out." One of those names was Gramme Laird. Unbelievably, we may be in the right area. I cried out to Jen.

We had initially planned to head over to Glasgow the following day but decided to divert and spend the night in Selkirk. It was about 10 miles south. According to the map, that appeared to be what we usually consider the county seat for the area. It was a commercial hub and included numerous schools, a hospital, and even a records office.

When we woke up the following day in Selkirk, I stuck my head out the window. It was a clear day, but there was a bone chilling wind blowing that is common this time of year. The small hotel was in a historic neighborhood with narrow, cobblestone streets. After walking a bit, we had coffee and dropped into a rustic old diner for breakfast. Our waitress kindly gave us a little background on the city and told us where to find the local cemetery and records office.

The cemetery was just a few blocks away, and we strolled down there and started checking out names. We have been to a dozen of these cemeteries and developed a system to cover the grounds efficiently. These old cemeteries date back hundreds of years. We found a lot of names dating back to the mid-1700s. The older ones become hard to read. I am starting to walk down the next row when I see it, 'Gramme Laird - 1918 to 1942". There is a headstone next to his with what appears to be another Laird. However, moss has grown into the inscription. The name is not discernable. Jen, showing her exuberance, shouts out "maybe we can clean it up so that we can read what's there." I responded "That's a good idea. But why don't we wait until after we go to the records office? Perhaps this information we are after is available there."

The records office opened at 11, so we waited anxiously at the door. We were filled with anticipation, feeling like we were on the verge of discovery. Those feelings were so thick that you could cut them with a knife. We spent all afternoon exhaustively sifting through record after record, and finally, there it was, "Jack, I found it!" Jen shouted out, showing a greatly heightened sense of anticipation. It was a birth record of an Elspeth Laird from a Roslin Laird, dated 1947. Within that discovery, however, there was no mention of a father. We could also not find any history of Tobias Laird, which would have connected Gramme to Jen. But we found a marriage record between Gramme and Roslin Laird a few moments later, dated April 11, 1938. "Wow, this is exciting!" Jen replied.

It was almost sunset as the record office closed. We decided to convene for the day and collect notes at this old pub just down the street from where we had breakfast. This pub was a relic, maybe a couple hundred years old, with rock walls, wooden beams, and aged dark furniture that looked handmade. A distinctive, almost musty smell seems familiar for these old places. Sitting at the bar, I told Jen that Glenn would love their Scotch selection. I only know a little about brands, except that older is better. You could tell by the dust that these bottles had been opened for a long time.

Behind the bar was this old, salty Scotsman with a deep brogue. He immediately commented on Jen. He said "Whit ye walked in, Ah thought Ah wis lookin' at an angel" [when you walked in, I thought I was looking at an angel]. Jen paused momentarily and then countered with a slight brogue of her own. What she said was surprisingly whitty for her. She said, "Whit self-respectin' angel wid come into a pub like this?" The bartender laughed and said "'Aye. An unfortunate turn of phrase on my part".

Now that Jen had broken the ice, this might be a good time to try out some of our canned Gaelic phrases. I uttered "Am faigh mi lionn" or something like that. The bartender laughed again and said, "I think you just asked me if I need a siùrsach [hooker]. The answer is Aye, but I'm guessing that's not what he meant to say." "Mo leisgeul," I responded, pulling another term from Jen's Gaelic phrases. "I understand that," the bartender said, smiling, pouring us 2 pints of their best lager.

"Whit brings ye to Selkirk?" the bartender asked as he pulled out a rag and wiped down the bar. Jen said "we are here from the US and are tryin to locate family in Scotland." "I've been here forever," replied the bartender. "Maybe I can help ye."

Jen explained that we were looking for a couple named Gramme and Roslin Laird, with a daughter named Elspeth. The bartender almost immediately responded in a manner that seemed hesitant to answer. "There's been lotsa Lairds come through here over the years. Sorry I can't help ye". He then went over and poured a drink for another gentleman toward the end of the bar. Jen and I then went back to reviewing our notes.

About 10 minutes later, the bartender returns and says, "Ye know, I went to school with an Elspeth. Her last name could have been Laird. A dinnae ken [I don't know]... What I do remember is that her mom (Roslin) was a real bonnie lass [attractive woman], and there was always talk of her being a lady about town if ye ken whit a mean." Jen smiled and replied in clear Gaelic, "Tapadh leat [thank you]."

We finished our pints and then proceeded to the door. As we walked out, the bartender stopped us and said, "I remembered one thing about Elspeth. She was a golfer and a damn good one at that.." Hmmm. I said to myself. This is getting interesting. Jen, with the buzz of all the discovery, was talking a mile a minute as we walked toward our room. She was nearly giddy with anticipation of what we may learn tomorrow.

We now know Gramme and Roslin were married, probably before Gramme went off to war. Gramme seems to have died in battle while Roslin remained in town. Nothing was found on Tobias. Elspeth was born, apparently out of wedlock, after the war. The bartender suggested Roslin was promiscuous, which might make sense. Jen then said, "Or perhaps she was just lonely." I nodded, acknowledging Jen's more sensitive, empathetic perspective.

We also know Elspeth was born in 1947, most likely grew up in Selkirk, and was even a golfer. I told Jen, "We have quite a bit to go on here." But Jen reminded me there were still a lot of questions. "The biggest thing is, we do not know what happened to Elspeth after she finished school. Did she marry? If she is still alive, where is she?" I responded, "It sounds like we should focus on Elspeth." Jen reminded me that an essential goal of hers is to determine how Tobias and Gramme are related.

I told Jen, "Something important here is that we know Elspeth is not the daughter of Gramme, which means you and I are not related. ". Jen got a curious look and nodded, indicating that the Tobias Laird connection to Gramme was no longer critical. Either way, the day's findings were fascinating and a reason to celebrate and reflect.

I can always tell when Jen is excited; she talks a lot. We were lying in separate beds this time, and she was talking a mile a minute about this possibility or that possibility. After a while, Jen finally stopped. After a pause, she asked me something totally random that came from way out in right field.

She asked, "Do you love golf?" I responded almost as a reflex, "I do." And then, assuming she wanted a long answer, I entered into a monologue. "I grew up a nobody, with nothing. I didn't have a home or even parents. I finally got comfortable and settled in with my foster family, and then I was off to someone else. That pattern repeated over and over again until I felt practically homeless, living in someone else's house. The golf game I discovered while living with Glenn is totally and genuinely mine. Nobody can take it away. That's part of it, but there is more.

A golf club feels like almost an extension of my body. People walk, and their legs know what to do. They operate automatically. I swing a golf club back and forth; it feels like my arms just know what to do. I know that sounds weird. I got this feeling of command over a ball that gave me a sense of confidence and stability I had never experienced.

Let me add one more thing. I spent a lot of my life in chaos, either in the middle of drug deals, drunks wanting to beat me up, or crime going down of all types. The golf course is void of chaos. It is calm, it is pristine, it is quiet. It is the place where I feel at peace."

Jen reached across the bed, squeezed my hand, smiled, rolled over, and turned out the light. "Goodnight Jack" she said. I lay awake for a spell, wondering what all that meant. The connection felt good.

The following day, we developed a revised plan. We agreed that we needed to focus on Elspeth with a deeper dive. Our first stop was the local newspaper office. We initially looked for articles on Elspeth Laird and came up empty. Jen then suggested we look for Elspeth and golf, and then a whole treasure trove of articles appeared. It seems like somewhere in her later teenage years, she went from using the last name of Laird to Gordon. We have yet to determine if that was related to marriage or something else. The articles indicate she was an accomplished golfer, winning the Scottish Women's Amateur in 1974, 1978 & 79, but nothing else. One tidbit noted Jen: her last Amateur win was in 1979, and she played at St. Andrews. "Let's go there. Perhaps somebody there remembers something".

Jen booked us a room at the Rusacks Hotel on the course at St. Andrews. Initially, I was uncomfortable with the expense, but Jen reminded me that she could afford it. It was a glorious place steeped in tradition. We walked through the halls and outside along the golf course. It was hard not to be in total awe of the golf tradition surrounding us. I explained to her that there was probably not a famous golfer who hadn't played there at some point in their lives. I did not understand it initially, but suddenly, the traditions of Old St. Andrews made sense. It was similar to Augusta National but much greater.

Throughout the area, we strolled into various shops and bars. Jen had taken her business card from work and added "looking for Elspeth Laird/Gordon" on the back. We handed those out where we could. As of now, I am still waiting for a response.

We finally stopped at a local pub once we saw one with a gray-haired bartender. We skipped pubs with young bartenders, figuring older ones were more familiar with the history. We sat down and ordered a couple of pints, and our first question to this burly gentleman was, have ye been here long? "Over 40 years," he stated proudly. I asked him if he had ever known Elspeth Gordon. She won the Scottish Amateur back here in 1979. He thought for a moment, then said, "Aye, and it's very funny you should ask. I've gotta story for ye", speaking with a strong brogue.

As Jen and I sat with amusement, he told us about his experience. "I did not follow golf much," he said. "But I got my first job here waiting tables about that time. I was waiting on a table over there", pointing to a table by the window. "There was this well-dressed man and a female golfer I had seen in the paper. She was the winner of the Women's Amateur. I was funlovin to the misses, nothing inappropriate, and the guy at the table thinks I am err chasing the lady's skirt, as they say. He gets up to confront me in a rage, and I walk away to avoid a fight. As I walk away, this guy takes a bottle from another table and breaks it over my head, giving me a nasty cut on the side of my head. I picked myself off the ground, and with blood running down the side of my face, I stumbled to my feet and told him I was going to have him thrown in jail. He then hands me 500 pounds and says, "Will this take care of it?". I said, "Sure. That was a lot of money back then. They walked out, and that was the last I ever saw of them."

The bartender said, "It turns out the guy who opened my head was a noble, err, a British aristocrat from the Carnoustie area. His name was Thomas Gordon, and I think he owned a golf course with Elspeth, his wife, or perhaps his ex-wife. That's all I ken tell ye." Jen handed him a nice tip and thanked him for the information,

Elspeth finally located

With the anticipation of getting closer to the truth, we swiftly checked out of the hotel and then made our way toward the coastline and Carnoustie, about 30 miles north. Like many places in Scotland, Carnoustie has a wealth of old historic castles, a historic town center, and multiple golf courses. As we have done previously, we found a room in the historic downtown proper with the plan to go seek out the local records office, visit a few local golf courses, and see if we can get closer to finding Elspeth's location.

We started walking around the town center and stopped and talked to a few locals. We settled into what appeared to be the oldest pub we could find. This bar was another of those ancient relics that Jen and I had grown to love in our brief week in Scotland. However, the bartender differed from some previous ones we had encountered. She wasn't crusty or old but was smartly dressed—maybe even modern—if that term applies to this section of the world. After she pours us a couple of pints, I ask her if she knows of a Thomas Gordan who lives in the area. I thought she knew him but seemed hesitant to speak of him. Jen then asks, "Do you know of an Elspeth Gordon, or it could be Laird?" she replies, "Sure." I think you are referring to Elspeth Laird. She comes in here frequently. "Nice lady," the bartender added. Jen asked if she knew where I could find her, and the bartender responded that she routinely volunteers at the women's shelter. You could probably find her there. It is located just around the corner." Usually, we finish our pints, but by this time, the excitement and anticipation level had us nearly running for the door.

We walked around the corner and located the women's shelter. Inside is a well-dressed, attractive, gray-haired woman sitting at a table, speaking to someone on the phone. It sounded like the person she talked to was distressed, and this lady seemed genuinely focused on her welfare. We waited with excitement for what seemed like an eternity. The lady at the table finishes her call and asks politely, "Can I help you?". "We are from the United States and are looking for Elspeth Laird. Do you know where we could find her?". "That be I," she explained as an incredible sense of relief came over us. Jen started out telling our story. Elspeth initially seemed skeptical and guarded but then opened up some. It became apparent from observing Jen's sincerity. Elspeth interrupted Jen briefly and said, "I am on duty here until 6. Perhaps we could meet for dinner. How about the Rookery?". Jen said, "Sounds good. See you after 6".

It was about a 15-minute walk to the Rookery, which borders the famous Carnoustie Golf Links. Over the years, numerous tournaments have been played at that course, even The Open on multiple occasions. We walked in and observed that the restaurant looked pretty exclusive. Elspeth had already reserved a table by the window overlooking the golf course. It seemed like she was a regular. We sat at the bar, waiting for Elspeth to arrive, bubbling in anticipation. Jen reaches over, grabs my hand, and says, "This is what we came all this way for." Tears came to both our eyes as we took in the enormity of it all.

Elspeth arrived on time, and the people there greeted her as an honored guest. We sit at a quiet table, and the maître d hands us napkins for our laps, then instructs our server to bring out Elspeth's favorite wine. "I hope you like this," Elspeth replies. We enjoy a glass of wine and cheese as she engages in small talk to break the mood and become better acquainted before delving into more intense topics. She speaks with a slight Scottish accent, but it is not a brogue. I would characterize it as lacking slang and more refined than most commoners.

Our waiter comes by and tops off our wine glasses. Elspeth now asks, "I would like to hear about your journey." Jen, clearly the most articulate of us two, started by describing our respective backgrounds and how searches for our ancestors took us to a 23andMe search that revealed Elspeth as a relative. Jen explained how we found her through a series of discoveries from a church in Galashiels to a pub owner in Selkirk who remembered her as a golfer from school. Newspaper clippings led us to St Andrews, where a bartender had a brush-up with Thomas Gordon.

"I assume you are the Elspeth Laird we have searched for," Jen responded. There was a pause where Elspeth then got an odd look on her face. If she wanted to exit the situation, Jen gave her the perfect opportunity. But instead, her face responded with a very gentile look. She replied, "Aye, that is I," seeing the noticeable relief on our faces. She then motioned the waiter to begin preparing dinner. As we waited, sipping the wine, she asked, "I am sure you have a thousand questions. Feel free to ask."

Jen wanted to learn about her involvement in the women's shelter. Instead, I interjected that it would be best to ask things in order. Jen nodded, and then I asked, "Tell us about Gramme." Elspeth said, "I never knew him. He died in the war before I was born. They married right before heading off to war, as many did. Mum was crazy about him and told me she was devastated over his death. "

Jen asked, "Did you know a Tobias Laird? He was a relative of Gramme. "Jen explained how Tobias was her relative and somehow linked to Gramme. "Our original notion was that we two (Jen and I) might be related." Elspeth smiled and said, "Since Gramme was not my father, that is probably not likely. Sorry, I did not know a Tobias Laird."

Jen then asked, "Do you know who your father was?" Elspeth responded, "Roslin didn't know or wouldn't tell me. After the war, Roslin said things were pretty crazy, and she found herself in situations she wished she could have taken back. Roslin died shortly after I got married and lived in a small cabin in the country not far outside Selkirk. After she died, we boarded up the place. Since then, I have not had the heart to go out there. "

I then ask, "So you were married. Was this to Thomas Gordon?". "Aye. Thomas was the son of an Earl. They owned a castle, an estate, and a golf course nearby. When I was young, Thomas was a golfer who saw me play in a local tournament and instantly fell in love with me. We had a whirlwind courtship with extravagance like I had never seen. There were estate dinners in the castle. We flew to Paris in their private jet. We played golf at posh resorts and country clubs. Our courtship lasted only a few months before we were married. Thomas was next in line to become Earl. After our marriage, he thought I needed special training to become worthy of a countess. I spent the following months in debutante training to learn how to speak and act with the proper dignity of the Gordon position. Shortly after that, Thomas' dad died unexpectedly. Thomas inherited new duties and responsibilities that sadly changed him. Even when we met, he could be irritated and mean, but that quickly transformed into violence and anger. He became insanely jealous and would beat me for anything that even approached insubordination. The beatings became excessive. One time, he even sent me to the hospital. His handlers would cover it up. Ultimately, I could not take anymore and divorced him in exchange for not pressing criminal charges. "

Elspeth then asks, "How is your venison?" We both respond with "Excellent," having never had it before but enjoying the local fare.

Still sitting on the edge of chairs, I ask, "What happened then?". Elspeth says that she then returned to playing golf. She said the divorce left her very well financially, and she had time and the opportunity to focus on her game. "I won a few tournaments." she said, "I followed that up with, "I would not call winning the Scottish Amateur 3 times, just a few tournaments." I said. "Did you have any thoughts of turning pro?" She said, "No. I was never trying to get my name in lights, but I found golf, and being out on the golf course brought me peace. "Jen and I looked at each other in total amazement, remembering that I made the same comment only two days earlier.

Jen then asked the question we had been waiting all evening to ask. "Did you have any children?" She said, seeming to change the subject, "I was intrigued by the waiter's story following the 1979 Women's Amateur. I had won the tournament and was unexpectedly accosted by Thomas, who begged me to get back together with him. Out of some strange sympathy, I agreed to talk to him. We walked over to the pub, and he used every tactic one could imagine to pull me back. Fortunately, I had the strength to say no. At about the same time, the waiter, I assume the one you met, responded to my distress. With that, Thomas became belligerent and hit that poor boy over the head with a bottle. I ran off and have never seen Thomas again. Later that night, I attended a party, got very drunk, and slept with some golfer who watched me play. I got pregnant and had Sheena."

"Was Sheena your only child?" Jen asked. "Aye, and fortunately so. I was not a good parent. I grew up without a father in my life. Sheena grew up without a father in her life. I think a father's love is something important in the balance of young women. I think it made be more jaded and less tolerant of men. I am not making excuses or suggesting I should have done things differently. I am just making a point."

The waiter then served dessert with a Cognac. "The dessert is called Cranachan. It is a Scottish delicacy." Elspeth said.

"What happened to Sheena?" I ask with heightened anticipation. She was a good golfer and got a scholarship at a university in Georgia. She married some guy, got pregnant, and I have not heard from her since." "Didn't you want to try to find her?" Jen asks. Elspeth then responded with something important. She said, "Sheena and I parted on terrible terms. Some might even call our relationship toxic. And I take credit for much of that. But after she left, I felt very broken, probably due to my relationship with Thomas Gordon. I finally healed myself by working at the shelter and playing golf with my lady friends. I thought reaching out to her might be a psychological setback for us both."

We finished a wonderful meal and exchanged pleasantries along with our respective email addresses with the hope that we could continue to correspond. On the way out, the Maître d handed me a bottle of 18-year-old Macallan. He said," This is compliments of Ms Laird. It is a particular Scotch from our Spey region just north of here." Jen, who distributes Macallan in the States, says, "Do you realize that is a $400 bottle of Scotch?".

Jen and I were both exhausted from the enormity of the evening, not to mention we were a wee bit intoxicated from all the alcohol. After leaving the restaurant, we decided to walk along the oceanfront. The full moon was out, and it was an unusually calm evening. Jen then suggests we pull out the Scotch. "We probably can't take it home anyway". We each start taking swigs out of the bottle, transitioning to a much higher state of intoxication.

Jen replies with a noticeable slur, "If she is your grandmother like we both think, then you have one hell of a family." Jen then says to me something that rarely exposes her inner feelings. "Jack, you should know something. This trip has been the most wonderful week of my life. I really needed this time together to clarify my feelings for you." she said. She then turned toward me and kissed me passionately like I had never been kissed before. We went back to our room and made love that lasted till morning.

I woke up the next morning with sea air blowing in the window and the sun beaming in my face. Jen is lying next to me. I was absolutely glowing inside.

I kept looking at her as I reflected on the previous evening. I almost cried as I absorbed the grandeur of this incredible woman. She looked so angelic lying there, and there was a subtle curve in her smile, much like the Monalisa. Jen's smile reflected a newfound sense of contentment and a peace that I think has eluded her over the past months. The only thought that could explain my projection of her is that this women I love is perfect.

Does it get any better than this?"

Our Last Day in Scotland

Jen woke up an hour later. I had already walked to the coffee shop and picked her up a coffee and a rowie. A rowie is something like a scone. I also brought her flowers and set them on the table. She woke up looking very content. I asked her how she was feeling. "Really good, headache aside" she said as she sat down eating her rowie. After about 10 minutes of silence, I asked her if last night was about the alcohol or if it was something different. She said, "The alcohol was a small factor," showing a bit of a sly smile as she said it.

She then grabbed my hand and said something I had been waiting to hear for nearly a year. She said, "After Grams died, I wondered if our high school relationship was something real and lasting or just a high school fling. I knew if I jumped back in the fire with you, I would get emotionally entwined and never be able to answer that critical question. This week with you has shown me our love is real and sustainable. It may be a long drop, but I am now ready to jump off the cliff with you, Jack Jeffers. "she said.

I was blown away by Jen and unable to express my emotions. I reminded her of something I had said before. "I have loved you from the first day I saw you walking down the fairway. I will always love you and will never waver. "She led me over to the bed and pulled me on top of her. We made passionate love for several more hours until we were interrupted by an anxious house-cleaning staff.

We agreed to spend our last afternoon in Scotland around the Old Course at St Andrews, walking around, taking in the scenery, and mingling with the locals. As we walked along the course, we talked about its history and how it represents the center of the universe as far as golf is concerned. Being totally consumed with the majesticness of the place, I then mused with Jen about how I would love to play in The Open Championship someday with a half-serious tone. Jen then said something I will never forget. "Many people have dreams, but except for a rare few, those dreams are just dreams. You are special, Jack Jeffers. You have overcome every challenge placed in front of you. If you really want and believe in your heart that you can play in The Open, you will. I believe it at my core", grabbing my hands and shaking them.

We walked for a while longer, then dropped into the pub for a pint. We sat down, and the waiter who helped us find Elspeth came over to say hi. We explained how his tip led us to find her, and we owed him a lot. He quipped, "I owe you as he instructed the bartender to pour us a couple of pints. Yours was the biggest tip I had received all month. Jen explained to him that I plan to be playing here someday in The Open. The waiter laughed, as this is not uncommon bar talk they hear often. Jen said, "Jack is the 3rd ranked amateur golfer in the world. His eyes suddenly changed, and he realized this was not just bar talk.

A few minutes later, a nicely dressed gentleman in golf attire came over to our table and introduced himself. "I understand you want to play in The Open Championship." I said, "I do, sir." "Is it true that you are the 3rd ranked Amateur in the World?" "Yes, he is," Jen said authoritatively, "...and he has only been playing for two years". "That is astonishing," the gentleman said. "I tell you what. If you get to number 1 by June 1 or you win the US Amateur" give me a call. I will get you in." He handed me his card, which indicated he was affiliated with The Royal and Ancient Golf Club of St Andrews. He then went back to his table. Jen and I looked at one another, and Jen said, "Jack you can do this."

Chapter 10

Jack Finds his Parents

We arrived back in Georgia feeling renewed on many fronts. I had a long download session with Glenn, covering the incredible experience of the past week. I went through our search and how we found Elspeth. I also told him about how Jen and I had recaptured our love. In reaction to my incredible emotional outpouring, Glenn had another classic response that seemed to sum up everything that happened in Scotland. "So what you are saying is that you missed me." I just had to laugh.

I told him that now Jen and I were back together and that we would be spending some 'sleep-overs.' He had another Glen-esk response: "Great. Just keep the noise down".

We are starting the following Monday, and classes at GT resume from the Spring semester. We originally planned on starting our search for Sheena at Georgia Tech, where Jen could use the Law Library and LexisNexis. Unfortunately, that service has now been blocked from non-Law students. Instead, we started with basic Internet sleuthing to see if that would take us anywhere.

I also hatched another idea. Elspeth said that Sheena has a scholarship offer from a Georgia university. I have cards from men's coaches and will ask them if they could do me a favor.

There is a Sheena Laird who was an essential person in my past that I need to find to connect the ancestral dots. She received a golf scholarship offer back around 1999. Do they know what happened to her or where she went?

Glenn suggests we contact a detective. They are experts at locating people. I was concerned that if Sheena discovered that people were looking for her, she might go into hiding so that we might never find her. I told Glenn, let's keep that idea in our hip pockets if we strike out elsewhere.

A few weeks passed, and we found no clues using social media or normal Internet look-ups. We searched for normal things like marriage or death records.

We were getting discouraged and considered hiring the detective like Glenn suggested when I received a text from Augusta University, formerly Augusta State. The text provided a number and said to call this lady, their former coach, around 20 years ago. She has information that might be helpful. I instructed Coach Blue from Augusta that he was the only one to respond to me, and I value his help. I would find a way to repay him. He said I could play golf for Augusta U. I laughed and thanked him.

Jen and I put in a call to the former women's coach. She had a wealth of information and seemed somewhat guarded to talk but was mainly extending Coach Blue a favor. The coach said that they were highly excited about Sheena joining her team. However, when she came in, they believed she had a substance abuse issue. Her substandard performance in her schoolwork made it easy to pull the plug on her. After she left Augusta, we heard she was working at a golf instruction center at Hilton Head. She closed with a couple of added remarks. She is talking to me as a favor to Coach Blue, and she would deny the content of this conversation if ever asked. BTW, she said, "Sheena was an incredible golfer. Maybe even national title contender caliber. "

That weekend, the RBC Heritage Open was being held at Hilton Head, but I decided to venture down there anyway to visit a couple of the instruction centers in the area. The first center had only existed for about ten years, and they had never heard of her. The 2nd instruction center was much older. I was told I needed to talk with David, who has been the owner since the outset. Unfortunately, he was at the tournament, but I told the attendant I would wait.

Eventually, he walked in around 4 pm and saw us waiting. He reluctantly agreed to speak with us, claiming he only had a few minutes. He mentioned that he was acquainted with Sheena, who used to frequent this place in search of an instructor job. She was an excellent golfer, but I was always suspicions if she was under the influence of something. Eventually, she got involved with one of our instructors and left soon after. Later, I discovered that this instructor worked at a golf shop in Atlanta after filing for unemployment benefits. I want David to disclose the instructor's name and the golf shop where he worked. It seemed apparent that he had no intention of helping me out.

At that moment, Jen inquired if the owner had watched any of the Jones Cup tournaments last fall. The owner confidently replied, "Of course. I had several golfers from my school participating in it." Jen asked if he knew who won, to which he responded, "Oh, it was some kid from Atlanta." Jen then cleverly gestured towards me. The owner's face lit up like a candle as he exclaimed, "No shit! That was an incredible performance." He then asked if he could introduce me to some of his students, mentioning how they would be thrilled to meet me. Just as I was about to agree, Jen interjected, "Let me propose a trade, the introduction, in exchange for the information about the instructor." Reluctantly, he said, "OK," acknowledging the deal.

He walked into the back office and came out about 10 minutes later. He had a name, Cole Costen, and he worked at Gonzo Golf in South Atlanta. That was precisely what we needed as we walked to the practice area. When we got there, we met about a half dozen golfers. One of those players was on my 1st day, 3-some. Unfortunately, I did not remember him. I felt bad. Still, I enjoyed shaking hands and extending some well-wishes and a golf story or two. Most importantly, I got my info.

While there, we made our way to the RBC Open, held on the other side of the island. I got to see Jordan Spieth up close. He and I are about the same size, and I was amazed at how much more power he gets out of his body. Jeff, my instructor, and I have talked about this many times. He told me I could improve my swing speed with appropriate weight training. More incredible swing speed = more distance, he says. But, to add significantly to that swing speed, I need to make significant revisions to your golf swing, specifically to my extension and swing arc. The risk is that you may damage your consistency and accuracy irreparably. Until you decide to go professional, we agree I should ride the horse I am on for as long as possible.

On the following Monday, after classes, Jen and I drove over to Gonzo Golf to see what we could learn about Cole Costen. We walked in and asked for the manager. We introduced ourselves, and before we could make a request, the manager said, "I recognize you. You are Jack Jeffers, that golf phenom from East Atlanta. Is that you? "In the flesh," Jen says. We are looking for Cole Costen. It's nothing bad. He has some information that might be important to us. The manager responded, "I wouldn't normally, but since you are a golf god around these parts, OK."

We found Cole

We got a phone number and made contact with Cole. We asked if he would meet us, but he refused repeatedly. Jen then got a great idea. She countered with a generous financial inducement. He agreed.

We walked into the bar, and Jen recognized him immediately. She said, "Do you see those eyes?" I said, "Where?" "OMG," she said, instantly seeing how his eyes and my eyes were nearly identical. We all sat down, and the first thing he says is, "The money first." Jen dropped down three hundred, holding two more in her hand. Cole swiftly swooped the three into his pocket and said, "What would you like to know?"

Cole reminded me of guys I used to see on the street. In his day, I could see where he might have been good-looking and vibrant but now appears beaten down by life. His face was gaunt. His hair was long and unkempt. His clothes were decent but dirty. He had this blank stare on his face and an overall demeanor that seemed like someone who was generally pensive. My experience from the hood told me that Cole was just another junkie waiting for his next fix.

Jen asked Cole, "We are trying to find Sheena Laird. We understand that you may know something about her." "Ya, I know something about her," Cole said. "I was married to her a while back ."Jen then asks, what can you tell me about her?". "She was one hell of a golfer." He said.   But she had demons, ones I could never expel. When I first met her at Hilton Head, she was calm and just liked a taste here and there. [that is, she was an infrequent drug user].   After a while, I don't know what happened; we were both strung out all the time [on drugs].   After a month of marriage, I started worrying about her out-trading sex for junk. I could not take it anymore and kicked her out. I have not seen her since." I asked, "Do you know what happened to her?" I had heard that she overdosed a few years after we split and is dead. That's all I know." Jen handed him the two hundred she was holding in her hand. As we were walking out of the bar, I turned around and asked one more question. "Did you know Ashleigh Dickenson?" He said, "I had an older sister named Ashleigh. She was married about the time I left home. Haven't seen her since." We thanked him and departed.

On the walk out to the car, Jen mentions that Cole did not speak of Sheena being pregnant. I wonder if he knew. "That is interesting for sure," I replied.
.

Jen, Glenn, and I sat down and spun Glenn up on the bittersweet events of the day. "Here is what we learned, Glenn," I said, not knowing exactly how I should feel. I continued, "I am feeling numb right now, and it is hard for me to know where to go with this conversation. "Glenn leaned forward in his chair like he does when he wants to engage more with the conversation. I told him that it appears that Sheena died maybe a decade ago and that she was married briefly to a loser drug addict. "If I am related to either of these people, I feel like shit."

"Jack, people choose substance abuse because they can't deal with their life in other ways," Glenn said. I countered, "Glenn, I am not being critical here, but I am just trying to understand. You sit here each night with your Scotch. Isn't that kind of the same thing?" Glenn said, "My love affair with Scotch helps me relax. It keeps me chill, as you might say. I am not sitting here getting plastered every night trying to suppress pain in my life with alcohol. I have done that in the past and I know exactly what that looks like. I will tell you with honesty that I am not doing that now. And before you suggest that I might have a lot of pain to suppress, consider that sitting in my chair sipping on Scotch has been a part of my routine for decades."

"In Scotland, Elspeth ordered a lot of alcohol. I have to say that, frankly, this added a lot to the enjoyment of the evening. Is Elspeth abusing a drug? Are Jen and I headed down the slippery slope by engaging in that? "I asked.

Glenn added a lot of clarity when he described an important distinction between social enjoyment versus pain suppression. He also talked about compulsive behavior, where you are compelled to engage in drug consumption, even when it is not appropriate or enjoyable. He correctly pointed out that he generally drinks little at the Club, out on the course, or when he travels.

I think Jen and I get it. Glenn calls substances' false witnesses', using a biblical metaphor. They never provide the solution they promise. One thing he said to me that was important. If Cole and Sheena are your parents, you are probably predisposed to substance dependence. He said it is essential to have a heightened sense—almost like a radar—that detects when you are inappropriately using substances. It is important to not cross to the other side of the tracks.

Glenn helped me a lot. To use his expression, he is a wise old bird. I can now control whether substances are part of my life. Given what seems like my lineage of abusers, it is not necessarily ordained that I will also. But as Glenn suggests, we need to stay vigilant. Jen agrees.

Glenn then changed the conversation. He asked, "Where do you think you want to go with your parental search? "Where can we go?" I asked. Glenn said, "Ultimately, we need to unseal your birth records." My obvious response was, "How do we do that?". Glenn said that we can't use 23andMe findings to unseal birth records. We need to either find the death record for Sheena or establish that Cole is your biological father with a DNA test. We would then need his written permission to unseal. Of course, this all assumes they are your parents."

Jen, who had stayed pretty quiet, finally chimes in, "Now that I know Sheena's last name could be Colson. I will see if I can find a death certificate." I responded, "We probably need that, Jen, because I can't see Cole giving us permission for anything." Jen had a different take. "I think Cole will give us anything we need. We know he can be bribed," Jen argues with a subtle smile.

Jen takes off to attend to some personal matters. Glenn tells me, "I had something I wanted to discuss with you." Whenever Glenn says, I know something important is coming, either good or bad. What will it be this time? I sat and wondered.

Glenn, my legal guardian

Glenn tells me he had much time to reflect on our relationship while I was gone. He discussed how that relationship has been legally informal to date, but he would be interested in adopting me if that is something I might consider. Frankly, my head was still spinning after the events of the day. My first thought was to question Glenn's timing. After a moment, I cleared my mind to ask a relevant question. "What does that mean, exactly.?"

Glenn started, "Jack, this would be a legal contract between you and me, and as a lawyer and a party to a potential agreement, it would be inappropriate for me to advise you. If you could consider this, you will want to seek your own legal counsel. That said, I will say that you are no longer a minor and are free to make your own choices as an adult. In a nutshell, this changes our foster parent-child relationship to one that is father-child. As my non-biological child, you would have responsibilities to me per se, which would include having legal jurisdiction over my welfare if I was unable to take care of myself. You would be my sole heir when I pass. The biggest thing is that this codifies our ongoing relationship and my commitment to you. Throughout your history, I know you have lived without parental security. We have talked about how you lacked permanence and stability. I want to give you that permanence and stability. I want you to be able to call this 'your home' officially".

After hearing Glenn's words, my demeanor dramatically changed. Glenn said a lot of stuff. Some made sense; some didn't. What I did hear beyond the words is that Glenn really cares about me. Enough that he wants me to be a permanent member of his family. His son. Wow. And I tried to say something to add some levity to the discussion; I countered with, "Glenn, and I thought you were anxious to get rid of me." cracking a smile as I spoke something out of Glenn's playbook. "Quite the opposite, actually, Jack," Glenn said.

I then said something to Glenn that I often thought about but always struggled to communicate: "Glenn, I can never repay you for all you have done for me. You brought me here as a messed up kid. You were real to me. You showed me a better life I could never have imagined." I actually got teary-eyed as I spoke, holding back what felt like a total emotional meltdown about to happen. "I would be honored to be your son." I finally lost it. I was bursting out in an all-out cry. I reached over, hugged Glenn, and told him, "Thank you." He guardedly reciprocated the hug, like he does. I did notice he seemed a little misty, which was very unlike Glenn. His facial expressions spoke more toward his feelings about me than any of his words could convey.

After we broke off the emotionally-ridden embrace, he put his legal hat back on. He told me he would put together some paperwork for me to review. I think Jen has some legal counsel she has used and respects who can adequately advise you.

I went upstairs and lay in bed, reflecting on the day's events. What a whirlwind day, I thought to myself. From meeting my possible loser or a father to learning of the death of my probable mother to hearing Glenn's desire to be a permanent father. I also need to update Elspeth on what we learned today. That is going to take a lot of work. The day was just a lot to take in. Whew!

With my thoughts embroiled in family matters, I changed my pants to some more comfortable sweats. As I picked up my pants off the floor, my wallet fell out, with some cards and small papers inside. As I put them back, I noticed the card from the gentleman we met from The Open Committee. My brain suddenly moved from being reflective to being anxious. "Shit!" I shouted out loud, realizing I had an important golf tournament in three weeks. It's been a while since I have touched a club; I better turn my focus there ASAP.

I decided to turn it in early so I can get an early start tomorrow with a renewed sense of urgency.

Chapter 11

Pressure Builds as US Amateur looms

George L Coleman Invitational

After nearly a month off, I have turned my focus to the George L Coleman Invitational held in Augusta. The invitational is a 54-hole event played at the prestigious Augusta Country Club, only a few miles from Augusta National. It has a rich history of hosting the world's top amateurs. Past winners include legends such as Hal Sutton, David Duval, Stewart Cink, and Matt Kuchar. Bobby Jones also considered this along with East Lake, his home course, before building Augusta National, home of the Masters.

To date, I have yet to experience pressure in these tournaments. These were just me doing my thing. Of course, I wanted to win, but if I didn't, I would not jump off a bridge or anything. This tournament is different in that regard. I would love to return to Scotland and play in The Open Championship. In order to do that, winning this tournament is imperative.

The pressure is building.

The best way I know how to prepare is to get back into a regimen. On non-school days, I hit range balls in the morning, short game practice. In the afternoon, I play a practice nine, hit range balls, and then do more short-game practice at home. On Saturdays, I have a lesson with Jeff and then work on weak areas.

My first lesson since returning is tomorrow, and I am especially anxious about it. I need Jeff to ensure my swing is still aligned after the long lay-off. Jen agreed to hang around with me. She brings me energy and is steady when I need it. I enjoy having her be a part of my team.

Over the next week, she was especially engaged in my preparation. She took notes and made me think about what I was doing. Oftentimes, I seem to go through the motions. Jen tries to make me more present during practice. She will ask me questions about why I did this or why I did that. It forces me to think about what I do. After some history, I never know when Jen will jump in and ask about my shot. That forces me to know how to respond ahead of time and think about what I am doing.

I am feeling ready as we head to Augusta. We picked up Tim along the way. I caught Tim up on our trip to Scotland and told him about the opportunity to play in The Open Championship in July if we can get this done. We also talked about the field in this tournament. It is the toughest I have faced yet. Three of the world's top 5 amateurs will be playing this weekend.

Day 1 of the tournament. I arrived at the practice range an hour early. I always loved the smell of fresh-cut grass. It's a great way to clear my mind before I start. As I lay in bed, I will mentally practice various shots and visualize putts going in. However, over time, it creates a lot of mental clutter. Spending time by myself on the range lets me mentally declutter and approach the first tee with a clear head. Tim reminds me. On the course, don't think, just do. I reflected on my comment to Jen back in Scotland, telling her my body knows what to do if I can get my brain out of its way. Given my style, the 7000-yard layout is challenging, but its many bunkers are an equalizer. You have to be accurate.

Team Jeffers breezed through the first day with a 67. That is just one shot off the lead.

On Day 2. I was in the afternoon group. The morning group had perfect conditions. However, a squall came through in the afternoon with high winds and rain for about five holes. The weather created havoc for everyone, and I took a couple of bogies that I usually wouldn't have. I finished with 69, 4 out of the lead.

On the final day, I felt this tournament was within reach but slipping away at the same time. Champions rise to the occasion, and this was my occasion. I started out like a champion, firing birdies on 1, 4, 5, 6 and 7. I kicked myself for the bogey on the tough par3, but I was happy with my four under 32 overall. I continued my hot hand on the 2nd nine, carding six straight birdies. On 17, I lipped out a 12-footer for par. The 36-hole leader was playing conservatively, which gave me an opportunity. He did card a birdie to close my lead to 2. At this point, I needed to play smart for one hole, and the tournament was mine.

On 18, the current leader put his tee in the right rough. That was going to be a difficult place to make par. On my tee shot,

I just needed to clear the fairway trap, and then the green became an easy target. I had considered using a lesser club and laying up for a moment, but ultimately, I chose the driver. Once I made contact with the call, I knew I did not hit it perfectly. I had no idea if it had cleared the trap or whether it went in. It was going to be close. As I walked up, I realized it plugged into the trap below the lip when I got to the ball. They call it a fried egg, where the ball is buried, and all you can see is a small piece, like a yoke. I needed help to advance the ball. All I could do was stand at the top of the trap, bend way over, and swing hard, hoping for something good to happen.

The hard swing got the ball out. However, at the same time, the contorted stance caused me to pull a muscle in my back. I felt it right when it happened, and it hurt like hell. In the meantime, the previous leader hit a miraculous shot onto the green. I thought, shit, how did he do that? I had my own problems, however. I tried doing some stretches to loosen up the back, but it just wasn't going to happen. Usually, I would have hit a wedge onto the green, but instead, I took out a 3-wood with the hope of just using my arms to punch the ball between the traps and onto the green. It went about 135 yards into the bunker. I gutted out my bunker shot 10 feet away from the pin, wincing in pain. The previous leader drained a 20-foot putt. Even standing up to putt was difficult. I finally had to putt on my knees and missed the putt I had to have by 2 feet. I barely made the 2-foot putt from my knees, having to be helped back to my feet by Tim. All I could think about was that I lost by a fucking one stroke. Damn!

Jen wanted to stay for the ceremony afterward, but I insisted we hit the road. It was an exceedingly long, quiet drive back to Atlanta. I lay spread out in the backseat while Tim drove. Everyone was obviously disappointed. But at the same time, we know I did everything possible. Sometimes, in golf, you look for answers that explain strange outcomes. But at the end of the day, all golfers are subject to the whims of the golf gods. Had the golf gods carried my tee shot just 2 yards farther on 18, this Jeep would probably be celebrating.

Glenn tells me the golf gods frequently humble even the greatest golfers from time to time. Don't seek revenge. It is best to file it away and move on.

I spent a day in Glenn's hot tub rehabbing my back. I was worried that I had hurt it permanently, but given the improvement, it will be OK with a bit of rest. Later that evening, I decided to check out the World Rankings, and I was still number 3. Glenn reminds me that 2nd place in this big tournament was still pretty damn good. Still, I agonize over just how close I came.

Glenn keeps asking me, "How's your back?" almost to the point of annoyance. I tell him it's fine, it's fine. Yet, the various pained expressions and winces I make tell him a different story.

After about a week of it, Glenn said, despite my reluctance, we will see a specialist. He set me up with an orthopedic doctor who specializes in golf-related injuries. When I got to the appointment, we carefully reviewed how the injury occurred. He took routine X-rays and such and had me do some unusual stretches. After sitting in the waiting room for about half an hour, he came back with his diagnosis.

He said, "Fortunately, I am not seeing any damage to the cartilage. It appears that you have strained the quadratus lumborum muscle." pointing to an area toward my lower back.

The remedy is to rest with gradual stretching. Jet baths can help as well. "How long before I can play golf?" I asked in a concerned voice. "My best guess would be about six weeks, but it could be longer," the Orthopedist said. "OMG," I replied. "I've got US Open qualifiers in 3 ." The Orthopedist then said something, "I need to tell you something important." he said. "You risk having chronic problems with your back if you attempt to use it before it is adequately healed. These kinds of injuries have ended many professional golfing careers. I know you are a young man who is used to healing quickly. But I strongly urge you to take this seriously and to be extremely patient."

On the drive home, Glenn could tell I was anxious and disappointed. He asked me multiple times if I planned to take the doctor seriously. Originally, I just grumbled. But Glenn was pretty emphatic until I gave him an affirmative response. I finally agreed. "Yes, I will take him seriously," I said with a tone that I just wanted to be left alone. Jen came over, and Glenn was working on her. To my chagrin, Jen took this very seriously and made it clear that I would have to go through her to get back on the course before the doctor said I was ready.

US Open and Rehab

While everybody was on the 6-week rehab schedule, in the back of my mind, I thought I could be ready in time to play in the US Open qualifier. Unfortunately, I had made a pact with Glenn to not attempt to swing until the doctor cleared me. I diligently followed my exhaustive rehab regimen. After a while, I started to feel more active.

After a few weeks, I convinced Glenn that I felt good enough to begin practice for the 18-hole qualifier next Tuesday. Glenn, OK, but our deal was to get the doctor's OK first.

The next day, we got in to see the doctor. During his exam, he began with what almost seemed like massages of the muscle area. He says that it feels much better. My mood instantly improved, feeling like there still may be hope for next week. He then stood me up and placed me in this unusual stance. He then said, "I want you to swing very slowly." I swung back very slowly as instructed. The backswing was easy and painless. My first reaction was that I got this. Then, on the downswing, I got down just past the point where you would make contact with the ball. I then felt this excruciating wince in my back that forced me to drop the club. The doctor said, "If you start playing before that muscle is ready, you will experience that wince during your swing. It may not seem significant at the time. However, your body will correct to avoid the pain and change your swing in ways you may not discern. Trying to avoid any psycho-retraining is what we are trying to prevent."

At that point, once I accepted that the US Open was not going to happen, I realized I needed to treat this seriously and patiently. Still, it would take a lot of work to watch the US Open and not feel like I should be competing against the best.

During the next week, I struggled internally about whether to watch the tournament. The Pebble Beach course was gorgeous, but those narrow fairways, that deep rough, and the little greens would be challenging. I lamented about not being there for a bit, but then I saw Tiger struggle and miss the cut and knew I had made the right choice.

After a couple more weeks of diligent rehab, I started working on my short game at the house. To be safe, I continued for the next month, pledging to follow the doctor's orders until after the British Open.

I had much more anxiety over the British Open than I thought I would have. A few days before the tournament, I exercised and watched the Kevin Costner movie "Field of Dreams ."In this episode, he and Terrence Mann go to a baseball game at Finley Park in Boston, where they hear the voice tell them to "Go the Distance!". That leads them both to meet Moonlight Graham, who as a young ballplayer came so agonizingly close to his dream but saw it pass by like a breeze in the night. Glenn then reminded me of the key moment in the episode. Kevin Costner suggests to Dr Graham that it was a travesty that he got so very close to your dream but did not fulfill it. Dr Graham then counters with something meaningful. He says, "If I had only gotten to be a doctor for a day...now that would have been a travesty".

Glenn responded, "Jack, about the time you start feeling like a victim is the day you are defeated. Moonlight Graham may have lamented about his lost opportunity. Still, rather than feeling sorry for himself, he redirected his passion into becoming a doctor, which was incredibly valuable to his small town." Glenn added, "Let's not lose sight of what is important."

I am unsure why, but I spent much time reflecting on those comments. Glenn was right. I saw myself as a victim, but after some serious reflection, I acknowledged that there were probably much bigger things in the world than golf and that I needed perspective.

Glenn didn't talk much, but usually, when he spoke, his words were worthwhile. This was especially true in this case.

The following week, we consummated my adoption. I was officially Jack Andrews, although we all agreed that I should keep my existing name while I was still a competitive golfer. Name recognition is an important part of your brand. It is essential part of gaining opportunities.

We planned a huge celebration BBQ at the house to honor Glenn's newest family member. Glenn invited many of his people from his legal practice whom I had never met. We also invited Jeff and Tim from the Club and several others with whom Glenn had a long-standing relationship. It was highly festive and energizing. I was, frankly, shocked at how Glenn was so social. He was almost like a different person in some regards. I jested with him later about being the life of the party today, whereas he is usually so sober and restrained. He says he puts on a party hat now and then. I laughed. My favorite part was Glenn's toast to the newest member of his family. Glenn did a lot to make me feel special that day.

A couple of weeks after the British Open, I finally got cleared by my doctor to resume practice. The US Amateur championship was a little more than a month away, and I wanted to get my game back to a competitive level for that event.

I was also wrapping up summer school. I took a full load with the thought that it would be a pleasant diversion to golf, plus they had excellent facilities at school for physical therapy. It was also a time when I got to see Jen. She was mired in some work projects and could not get out much. It allowed me to drop by her work and visit or have dinner if time permitted.

Jen was coming up empty on the Sheena search. "That could be as expected," I asserted. We concluded, however, that if she was homeless or someone who overdosed, they may not have been able to identify her. We were resigned to the possibility that Sheena was lost forever.

Jen then came up with another idea. "Perhaps we could coax Cole into allowing us to test his DNA." If we could prove he is your biological father, then we are nearly assured Sheena is your mother beyond all else. We had initially agreed to put this on hold until our schedules were free, but Jen said, "Let's just do it."

To date, we have been unsuccessful in locating anything definitive–like a death record–for Sheena Colson. I had promised Elspeth that I would update her if I received any news. Admittedly, I have been putting it off, but I finally texted her with the news about Sheena. I reminded her that we had not found anything yet and that our news came from a dubious source, although he was her former husband. I also told her we were still looking and would let her know if additional news surfaced. She texted me without much of a response. "Thanks for the update. "she wrote. I'm unsure how to read that, but it's OK.

A few days later, Jen texted Cole and told him we needed a favor. Jen told me Cole quickly responded and reminded her that favors still cost $500. Jen said to him that she would give him $750 with the understanding that he could not ask why we were asking this favor. His first reaction was, "You aren't going to ask me to shake down a pimp, are you?". Jen explained it is nothing illegal or harmful to you. We can conclude our business in 10 minutes without leaving the bar." He agreed, and we met at the previous bar in South Atlanta.

We all sat down. Cole looked down and out just as we had been before. In fact, he was wearing the same clothing as the last time we saw him. Jen started talking, then Cole abruptly interrupted and said, "$750 please". Jen pulled out the money and sat it on the table. Cole reached for it, but before he could grab it, Jen pulled it away and said, "First, the favor." I handed him a saliva swab from 23andme, which he reluctantly put in his mouth. I then gave him this release form that permitted us to use his sample. I pulled out some scissors and told him I would cut a few hair strands. "You'll never miss it," I said. Cole got this angry face and replied, "What the fuck? What do you want this shit for?" Jen then reminded him of our deal where he could not ask about our purpose. He then got this resigned look and said, "OK." I reached over, cut a few strands, and put them in a plastic sack.

"Thank you," Jen said while sliding the money over to Cole. Jen then asked Cole something else. Do you have any of Sheena's belongings? "His eyebrows raised as he suddenly remembered that his mom might have kept a box of her stuff that she never picked up. Jen told him that if such a box provided something genuine and verifiably Sheena's, that would be worth $1500. He said, "Great." I will see what I can find. We got up to leave, and Jen spoke to him one more time. She said, "Cole, let me remind you that if you try to scam us, our business relationship is over." Jen had a way of being extremely convincing when she needed to. He nodded, and we left with what we came there for.

About a week later, Jen gets a text from Cole saying that he found the box at his mom's that he thought comprised

Sheena's stuff. We arranged a meeting at the same spot to review the contents.   Cole walked in with a medium-sized box that a casual observer might call junk. He sat at the table and asked, "Where's my $1500?". Jen said, "We need to make sure there is something here that is convincingly Sheena's and not just a pile of crap you picked up at the Goodwill."

We began rummaging through the stuff. It consisted of a couple of blouses, a bra, some make-up, a crown, a veil-like thing you would see in a shotgun wedding, and a couple of books on golf and golf instruction.   Jen said I still find nothing here proving this stuff is hers. I opened one of the golf books, and some pictures fell out. One was a wedding picture with a guy in a shirt and jeans. The bride was a red-haired girl, and she was wearing the crown and veil, like the one in the box. I asked Cole if he knew this couple, and he said, "Ya, that is Sheena and me." "There ya go, there ya go," Cole excitedly replied. "I told you I wasn't going to scam y'all." Feeling very good about what we found, Jen slid over the $1500 and said, "It has been a pleasure doing business with y'all."

Later that evening, we began combing through the box carefully. Jen had already sent a sample of Cole's saliva to 23andMe. If there was a DNA sample in this box, we could prove Sheena is Jack's mom without getting into the legal challenge of unsealing birth records. We had spent over an hour painstakingly going through each item in the box with a high-intensity lamp without luck. I then moved the wedding crown and veil under the lamp. As I looked under the crown, I saw a small red hair wedged behind one of the screws holding the piece together. "We found it!" I cried out. We carefully placed the sample into a small test tube the DNA sampling company provided.

Now we wait.

US Amateur

Since we have come to a logical stopping point with the ancestry search, it is time to urgently turn my attention to preparing for the US Amateur golf championship. This year's tournament is held at the stunning Pinehurst Resort and Country Club in North Carolina. I have never been, but the pictures I've seen make the place look jaw-droppingly amazing. Over the years, this golf course has hosted numerous high-profile events, both professional and amateur.

The US Amateur Championship spans six days and is widely regarded as the world's most prestigious amateur golf tournament. It has a long and illustrious history that dates back to 1895, with winners including Bobby Jones, Jack Nicklaus, and Tiger Woods.

In preparation for the event, I have been exceptionally careful and patient with my rehab. With the tournament only days away, any setback at this stage would likely doom my chances.

Since I returned from the disabled list, I have cut way back on the number of ball strikes on the range. The intent has been to avoid stressing muscles that may still not be 100%. The upside is that it has let me focus much more on my short and wedge games and work on course management skills. Jeff says my swing looks as good as it ever has. I am feeling healthy and refreshed going into the tournament. I should be ready.

I asked Jen if she receives any information on either Cole or Sheena, if she would sit on it until after the Amateur. While I am good at tuning out noise, the last thing I need is that distraction.

Tim and I decided to go up Pinehurst a couple of days early. Tim wanted to spend time reading the greens. I wanted to ensure I was dialed in on the grass and other playing conditions. Arriving early also allows me to get acclimated and comfortable before the tournament begins. Jen has a critical board meeting and will fly up in a few days.

The first two days are medal play. The top 64 performers of that round qualify for single-elimination match play. That will be a brand-new experience. But first things first.

Day 1 and 2 of medal play. The top 64 is easily within reach, barring a total catastrophe. The more significant issue is that I remain healthy. At the same time, I also need to get as high a seed as possible. Higher seeds have an easier path during matchplay.

My game was sharp on both days. I wasn't taking risks and was playing pretty conservatively overall. I carded a 68-68, which was good enough for 4th. This course was hard and long, spanning a distance of 7500 yards. My extra work at shots from 150 in really helped.

I took us to the Maxwell course for match play the next day. This is a shorter course that requires precision and ball placement. This course matches my skill set very well.

I despatched my early morning opponent 6-4. My afternoon challenger fell in a similar form, 6-5.

In the 3rd match, I encountered a player with a red-hot putter. He was draining everything inside 20 feet and had me sweating over the front nine as I was down 3. The following nine started slow, but I finally dialed it up and won the last 4 to finish 1-up. The 4th match was a near mirror image of the 3rd. I got down early but finished strong. I won 2-1, heading into the semi-finals.

Glenn called when I was driving to pick Jen up at the airport. He said he enjoyed watching me play on the tube and wished me the best over the next two matches. I enjoyed his call. The physical and emotional strain was admittedly wearing on me, and Jen being there gave me strength that I really needed for the final two rounds.

I told Jen about the day's events on the drive back to our hotel. I was describing to her something significant that occurred on number 9. I explained, "I had hit the ball over the green into this thick grass clump, like the ones on 11 and 13 at the Club. That is the only place I have seen this type of grass. But I know from experience that you think you can hit out of this stuff, but you can't. Tim and I elected to concede the hole rather than risk ending the tournament due to reinjury. That was hard to do, given the quality of the competition, but I am here rather than laying in traction somewhere." Jen grabbed my hand and smiled.

Championship Sunday was going to be grueling. There are two tough matches on the same day.

My semi-final opponent was an outstanding player. He was both long and accurate. This was another instance where I had to keep my ego in my shorts. He was constantly way beyond me off the tee, but with the help of Tim, I stayed in my lane.

We were even going into the long par five 16th. This hole was very reachable in 2 shots for my opponent. The best I could expect was to lay up and hope for a quality 3rd for a shot at birdie. He hit his drive into the woods while I hit into perfect position on the right side of the fairway. The opponent had to punch out, then hit a long 3-wood 15 feet away from the pin. I layed up and then hit a beautiful wedge off the pin for a tap-in birdie. My opponent left his put on the lip to put me 1-up with 2 to play. On par 3, 200 yards, 17th, I hit a 5-iron 6 feet away. Feeling he needed to make something happen, he pressed and left his shot in the trap. He approached the trap expecting that he needed to hole out to win, airmailed it over the green, and conceded the hole and the match, 2-1.

My final match this afternoon was going to be against the number 1 amateur in the US and the world. There was a huge gallery with TV cameras and media types all over. The buzz was almost deafening as I tried to compose myself for finals play in one hour. Jen, Tim, and I retired to the range, which afforded me some privacy and a little peace. I didn't hit my driver but just practiced easy wedges, attempting to stay loose.

I noticed my competitor signing autographs and talking with reporters on several occasions. I was alone and chilling on the range, which was closed to the public. That was a great move. I started like a firecracker while my opponent took a few holes to find his stride. I won the 1st four holes and was up five by the break. By the 10th hole, my body was aching, and I thought I could not wait for this to be over. Fortunately, despite the pain, I was able to string together some tough pars.

On the par three 12th hole, I had hit short and saw my tee shot back up off the green and roll down the hill. I hit my chip up the hill within 3 feet to halve the hole. On 15, I hit my tee shot short into the trap. Rather than trying to do too much with a tough lie, we elected to hit 20 yards backward to give me an open approach. The conservative move paid off. My next shot was a long 3-wood that I put 5 feet away, and I drained a must-have putt to win the Amateur 4-3 [up 4 with three holes to play].

Tim came over and hugged me as I walked off the green on 15. Then came Jen. "You did it", she said. And then, from hoards of people in the gallery, Glenn emerges. He had driven up that morning. "Congratulations, Son," he reached out, and we shook hands briefly; then I grabbed and hugged him. I told him, "I could not have done this without you." I walked the rest of the way to the scorer's table with my arm around Glenn. He beamed.

The rest of the day was an absolute fog. I remember laying flat on my back in the back seat, holding the silver jug, and looking at the winner's names dating back over one hundred years: Jack Nicklaus, Tiger Woods, and even Bobby Jones. Now Jack Jeffers. Wow!

A New Life

All it took was about eight hours for me to come to the realization that my life was forever altered. Alongside Glenn, Tim, and Jen, my photograph was plastered on nearly every newspaper in the region. I experienced some fame during my last year, but nothing like this. I couldn't go anywhere or do anything without running into someone who recognized me. What created an explosion of harassment were the pundits who assumed that I would turn professional, opening up a firehouse of agents, recruiters, and opportunists seeking to profit from me in the future. The situation became so overwhelming that Glenn and I could not go anywhere without being bombarded with proposals, offers, and even inducements. Individuals were quite literally throwing money at my feet.

One party who was a tremendous benefactor of my fame was Tim. His phone rang off the hook with professional golfers wanting to enlist him as their caddie. He found a great position as a caddy with an established professional. He did put one condition in his caddie employment agreement. He clarified that he would be my caddie at the Masters next Spring. Tim was a great asset to my team, and I will miss him. His loyalty and commitment to me is a quality I admire.

Even Glenn's legal practice enjoyed a bump. Glenn never worries about clients. He always claimed he had more work than he needed. Still, he enjoyed the elevated respect this all has brought him. Interestingly, the public now sees him as a golf specialist. He has gotten a dozen requests to provide legal advice on golf course-related matters. Even at the Club, you can tell he has elevated his standing. They are now using him for a land use issue adjacent to the course. He also enjoys the accolades among his members. They frequently approach him and chant, "That boy of yours is some golfer. He must take after the old man." Glenn just smiles and goes about his business. His golf calendar is uncharacteristically full.

Glenn had collected all the money people had left or sent us, hoping to secure a business relationship. The amount is close to $150,000, Glenn said. We obviously can't keep it and, in many cases, do not have a way to return it. Glenn called the USGA, who suggested that we donate it. Glenn came up with an even better idea. Let's set up a foundation. We will call it the Jack Jeffers Foundation, which will use golf to help disadvantaged youth rise out of their circumstances.

I always heard about foundations as I was growing up but never really understood them. Glenn explained it this way. "Think of it as a company, like Jen's distributorship. It has its own bank account and people who manage things. It even has its own office. Rather than distribute spirits, however, its sole purpose is to do good things for people, and because of that, the government gives it favorable tax status." Glenn says that he has set up many of these in his career. Not long after that, the Jack Jeffers Foundation was born.

Number 1 Amateur

I got a word with my US Amateur win; I was now the number-ranked golf amateur in the world. "Being the best in the world at something feels pretty damn good, Glenn." I lamented. "Glenn, have you ever known someone who was ranked number 1 in the world at something?" looking somewhat cocky. I put my feet comfortably upon the automan and told Glenn I wish I had a cigar.

Glenn's face suddenly shifted to seriousness, which usually signaled a lecture was in the offing. I mentally braced myself for what was coming. He said, "Before you think you are better than other people, look at José working in our yard. He probably knows more about caring for grass than you or I will ever know. In fact, he may even be the world's best in terms of yard maintenance. He is that good. Jack, you can't sing. You can't fix cars. Hell, you can hardly keep your room organized. My point to you is this, Jack. Stay humble. You have a special gift that has taken a long way, but you are hardly god's gift to humanity.

The Bible encourages us to nurture those gifts and use them for good. It's OK to feel good about your achievements. But remember, golf is just a game. For José, his passion is to work hard and feed his family. It's all a matter of relativity." He then started to put his reading glasses back when he stopped and said, "One more thing.
Awhile back, I told you that the first step to becoming wealthy is to understand what is valuable. You may not have known this at the time, but I was not talking about building a fat bank account, a large trophy case, or even getting headlines in the paper. My firm belief is that the greatest wealth in life comes from your relationships with family, friends, and God. At the end of the day, you will be judged more by things such as character, integrity, and what you give to this world than by accolades. My point is not to diminish anything you accomplished but just to give you some perspective."

After Glenn was done, I did not speak but looked at him sincerely. I think he understood that I understood his point and would carefully consider what he told me.

I spent the next couple of hours reflecting on Glenn's words and my life. I sat there watching José work tirelessly in the backyard. He cut the grass and trimmed the bushes. He meticulously manicured my practice green. He is not focused on fame or fortune, getting degrees, or sinking putts. His focus is on feeding his family. After sitting there and watching him, I got out of my chair and did something I had never done. I walked up to José and thanked him for doing such a great job on my practice green. He replied, "Gracias señor," and then went back to his work.

I emailed Elspeth, letting her know that I won the US Amateur and would be coming to see her next July at The Open Championship. She responded with her typical class and style "I always thought yer destined for great things. When you are in Scotland, you and your lass Jen, come stay here as my guest."

Largely in response to Glenn's advice, we agreed I needed to trample down the public's expectations regarding my plans. Glenn suggested a public statement in the form of a carefully worded press release as an excellent way to calm the 'he's turning pro' frenzy.

The press release went like this:

> I am grateful for all the support and encouragement the greater Atlanta community has shown me during my golf career. I have been incredibly touched–and moved–by how golfers–and even non-golfers–have embraced me following my win in the US Amateur.
>
> There has been wide speculation that my win last month would launch me on a new journey toward professional golf. I am announcing today that I am not planning to play professional golf for the foreseeable future, but will remain an amateur.

Instead, I will pursue my engineering degree at Georgia Tech and compete as a non-collegiate golfer. I will take some time off from golf, but then I will start diligent preparations for the Masters in the Spring.

Sincerely, Jack Jeffers

Even after the announcement, some would not accept my proclamation. Pursuing money and fame seems so apparent to some people that any other notion seems asinine. Fortunately, my press release quieted down most of the speculation. After a few weeks, things returned to something approaching normal.

I have realized that while I love golf and being a golfer, yet I think I want to be known for being more than just a golfer.

Cole and Sheena

During the Amateur Championship, Jen mentioned an important board meeting required her attendance. As a result, she came to the tournament several days late. We were having a late afternoon BBQ, and Glenn had a chance to catch up with her over what had transpired.

Jen said to Glenn and me, "This is confidential, but the board is interested in selling the company. We have been approached by a large national distributorship that wants to expand its reach into the southeast. They are making us an extremely generous offer. "Glenn then asks, "How do you feel about that?" Jen responded, "This company has been an integral part of my family for nearly 100 years. I feel that

Grams entrusted me to preserve this as a family legacy. At the same time, I have to be honest with myself. I am not sure this is my passion." Glenn adds, "Is there a way to keep the company that might still allow you to seek other options?" "Perhaps," Jen replies. "There is a lot of momentum steering us to sell, however. This position is being pushed mostly by a couple of outspoken parties who currently seem to be dominating the conversation. I am not sure if my voice matters." Glenn says, "It may matter more than you are aware. You should seriously enlist competent legal counsel to protect your interests, regardless of what they are." "Good advice, Glenn," Jen closed.

We all enjoyed a nice meal out on the patio. I smoked up some tri-tip and experimented with a new rub. I got a fantastic bark this time and was happy with it overall. Glenn has been turning me on to smoking meats. He tells me that it is a lifelong science of trial and error. Glenn follows that up with a great recipe for strawberry shortcake, and today's batch was excellent.

We retired to the air conditioning in the living room. Glenn stayed true to his routine as he settled into his chair with a glass of his favorite sipping Scotch. Jen then pulls out a sack with the results of the 23andMe search on Cole and the DNA test on what we thought was Sheena's hair sample. To lighten the mood, I barked out, "Drumroll, please." Jen opened the pamphlet that showed Cole's lineage. She then pauses to add a little intrigue, then smiles. "Cole is your dad," she said. I took a deep breath and then laid my head back. "Boy! I said, "That is a relief. it almost assures us that Sheena is/was my mom." Jen opened the envelope that compared Sheena's DNA from the hair sample to mine. "It shows Sheena is your mom," Jen said, confirming what we already suspected.

Glenn didn't show much emotion. He has been fairly silent over this ancestry search. Glenn doesn't play poker, but he is undoubtedly tough to read in this case.

My first action with the news was to text Elspeth and tell her I would now call her 'Wee Gran' or several other Scottish terms for grandmother. "I already knew I was. Gramma's intuition," she jested.

Jen and I were reflecting on the events of the day. "Whew, this has been quite a year," I mused. "Ain't that an understatement." Jen replied with an accentuated southern accent". As I sat there, I was hit with a sudden brainstorm. "What would you think if we tried to rehabilitate Cole?" Jen didn't even hesitate. "What a great idea!" she shouted. "Maybe a good initial project for the Foundation."

We brainstormed about possible ways to help him. Glenn interjected, "Have you considered that maybe he doesn't want help." Jen said, "We won't know if we don't ask." I then offered, "If we can get him clean, maybe he could help Jeff at the Club's learning center and build his resume as an instructor." Jen added, "I think Glenn is right. We need first to see where his head is. Let me reach out to him." I could tell by the look in her eye that this was something that had Jen energized. We both agreed that we did not want to tell Cole about being my father. Let's first build some mutual trust.

Jen texted Cole and set another meeting at our regular South Atlanta bar. Cole instantly expected Jen to open her wallet and lay out some cash. "Where's the money?" Cole exclaimed. Jen echoed, "No money this time. We are here to offer you something better. We want to give you a normal life if that is something you want." "Why would you want to help me?" Cole responded. Jen then came up with a clever yet nearly truthful answer. She said, "We are golfers. You are a golfer. That makes us like family, and we help family." "Well, OK," Cole said guardedly. "What do you want me to do?". Jen said, "The first thing we need you to do is get clean. We will send you to the rehab center. But you have to want to go. ". "I don't know if I'm ready for that," Cole said. "I'll think about it," and abruptly walked out.

We have yet to hear back from him. Jen characterized it well, recanting a biblical verse. "This is a great case where 'pride goeth before the fall .'I hope I am wrong."

Later that night, I reflected on her maturity and composure in working with Cole. She definitely has strong interpersonal skills and is passionate about helping others. I also have been thinking a lot lately about Jen and my relationship and wondering what my life might feel like without her. It did not take long for me to acknowledge that I did not want to imagine my life without her in it. I spoke to Glenn about my desire to ask Jen to marry me. I had no idea what Glenn would think. I know he thinks the world of her, but he might disagree with the timing, given we are both in school with our futures uncertain.

In the four years I've known Glenn, he has been known for a surprise or two. He surprised me once again. He responded, "I lived much of life waiting for stars to align. I have also seen that tomorrow is never a certainty." He reflected on his wife and son, who left this world too soon. "Jack, I think Jen is a wonderful girl. I have no doubt you will be happy together."

Glenn said. "So, does that mean I have your blessing?" I asked. Glenn responded, "Absolutely".

Glenn and I drove to the jeweler the next day and picked out a ring.

I called Jen and said, "Hey, Tomorrow [Saturday], I was thinking I'm anxious to get out to the course and play a few holes. Do you wanna go?" She said, "Sure".

I picked her up around 2, and we started by grabbing a late lunch. We went out to the range, and instead of going with my regular hitting regimen, we played some competitive games, like who could get closest to the flag from 100 yards. Jen could use any club in her bag. I had to use my driver. Jen was up 1 point, going onto the putting green. I won the putting leg by 1, which tied up our match. We then went onto the course, where she could use her entire bag, but I could only use one club. Jen chose that I use a sand wedge. She had the advantage in this one, but even though we were both competitive, that was OK. Jen definitely had the advantage and was 2-up after 2. The sun was setting, and the course had emptied except for the bag boys. I asked Jen to join me as we walked over to the particular spot on the golf course that looks out over the vista. This was also the place where Glenn had proposed to his wife.

As we stood looking out, I started talking to her in my warmest, most sensitive voice. I told her, "The last few years with you have been an incredible journey with both highs and lows. It has shown me how much you mean to me and how I cannot imagine my life without you in it. " I pulled out the ring, got down on my knee, and said, "I would be honored if you would be my wife." Tears streamed out of my eyes, and I held up the ring. Jen puts her hands up over her mouth, being in total surprise. She utters, "Oh My God," in a crackling voice, with her eyes visibly welling up. She paused briefly, attempting to gather herself. During that time, I nearly died as I waited for the answer that would forever change my life. She said, "Of course, I will". We hugged and kissed for what seemed like half an hour. As we walked back toward the clubhouse, I told her, "I will make you happy." She squeezed my hand and said, "I know you will."

We had a glorious walk-in, and we anxiously drove home to share the news with Glenn. On the radio in the Jeep, it played "Lucky Man" by Montgomery Gentry. The lyrics rang true with crystal clarity.

> But I know that I'm a Luck Man
>   God has given me a pretty fair hand
> Got a house and a piece of land
>   A few dollars in a coffee can
> My old truck is still runnin good.
>   My ticker is ticken the way they say it should
> I've got supper in the oven
>   A good women's love
> Another today to be my little kid's dad
>   Lord knows, I'm a lucky man

Damn, I am a lucky man.

Early today, I had instructed Glenn to act surprised when we walked in. Instead, he went off on some crazy thing with a tone of exuberance you would never see from him. "He already knew, didn't he?" Jen said. I smiled and told Glenn he was a terrible actor.

We explained to Glenn that we would like to have our wedding at the Old Course at St. Andrews. I already asked Tim to be my best man. Tim's fiance would be a great maid of honor. Even beyond the Amateur Championship, I consider this day the happiest of my life.

Cole's Rehab

It was a few months since we reached out to Cole, trying to offer him a life raft out of his drug-torn life. Following the meeting, Cole went silent. We assumed that he wasn't ready to take that step. I have heard that people with an addiction often need to first hit rock bottom before being able to accept help.

Cole had fallen out of consciousness when Jen received a call one evening. "Jen, I need your help. I did not know who else to call. People are chasing me. I'm strung out. I want to die. Please help," he begged. Jen and I entered the car and met him outside the Southside bar. He had overdosed and was going through some panic attacks. We rushed him to the hospital close to us, and they admitted him for an overdose.

The morning after, both of us had classes to attend. By noon, we escaped and hurried back to the hospital to inquire about his condition. However, once we reached the attending nurse, we were devastated to learn that he had already checked out. That was a real bummer.

I suggested to Jen that the best path is to leave him alone. She overpowered me, feeling compelled to at least let him know an open door was available to him. She texted with a little bit of tough love, "Please, do not contact us again until you are ready to detox." Glenn was there observing our interaction. He had a different idea. He said, "Jack. Have you ever thought of telling him he is your father?" I thought to myself, I would be scared to death to bring his shit into our home. But he is my biological father. I am not sure exactly how much I owe him, but I feel I owe him more than I have given so far.

Chapter 12

The Masters

I've had an intense fall semester of school. I am getting into the heart of my engineering courses. This semester, I am studying Differential equations, Statics and Dynamics, Fluid Mechanics and Computer-Aided Design. I have been a B+/A- student, which I am proud of, given my dubious academic history. I enjoy engineering, although I have yet to map out any kind of future in that discipline. Hopefully, that will materialize eventually. Jen is still taking business classes, but not with a degree trajectory.

With Glenn's help, Jen discovered that she has veto authority over any potential sale. She has made it clear to the board that there may be a time to consider a sale, but it needs to occur deliberately and in line with the firm's long-term objectives. Creating internal panic in reaction to the desperate overtures of any suitor is not sound decision-making in her view. When she showed me her response, I thought, 'Wow,' my Jen is something.

Jen and I decided to take a well-deserved break during the Christmas holiday after finishing our exams. Our destination was the Bahamas, where we aimed to relax and rejuvenate. I deliberately left my golf clubs behind, as my primary intention was not to indulge in the sport. Instead, I wished to unwind on the beach, take leisurely walks in the ocean, and cherish some quality moments with Jen.

After a highly relaxing week, we returned to reality, where the focus needed to be on school. Final exams were just a few weeks away. These would require my entire attention.

I am considering a lighter course load for the upcoming semester. I intend to allocate my undivided attention to golf in preparation for the Masters tournament in April.

It is the end of January, and finals are coming. They were challenging, but I am feeling good about the semester overall. A few days later, I discovered that hard work resulted in straight A's. When I can focus on school, I think I've got some academic chops.

According to plan, with school primarily out of the way, I can be laser-focused on preparations for the Masters. I am returning to the regimen that has worked so well for me. I will practice on the range in the morning, putting, short-game, and wedge-game at mid-day, followed by a practice round, then more range. At home, I will work on putting and chipping. The weather has been unseasonably cold, but my edge has been to practice steadily. Steady, consistent practice means continuous, consistent play. That's my hallmark.

I plan to defend my Jones Cup at the end of February. Depending on how I feel, I may try to get in one of the Florida tournaments in March as a tune-up before the Masters in early April.

Defending my Jones Cup

After a solid month of practice, Jen and I drove to Sea Island, Georgia, ready to complete. I am usually anxious going into these. Actually, I am almost always anxious. But I feel different this time. I am not worrying about competition or thinking about the course or strategy. Instead, I am focusing on myself and what I need to do. Even Jeff agrees that I have found a winning formula that involves staying in my lane and simply executing what I have trained to do.

Even with a solid plan, I must recognize that one factor is different this time. Tim is not with me. He is now the caddie for a hot-shot pro player. I am happy for him. But at the same time, Tim was uncanny at keeping me grounded with my head on straight. He could make me laugh and stay loose. He told me he was only there because I was too lazy to carry my own bag. I called Tim the other day and offered free advice for this tournament. He says, "When your head starts going wack, just remember what I would say. I thought, "Great. Like that is going to help." Jen suggested I might want to use an alternate caddie. I decided against that. I'm on my own this time. I have played the course three times now and feel comfortable with yardage and distances. Jen will also be there, offering her emotional support. At least there is no pressure to win this time. We will see how this goes.

Day 1 - I finished the day with a 2-under 68. I would characterize my golf as uninspiring. I didn't make any big mistakes. But at the same time, I played like someone who was not playing to win. I didn't attack the pin. I didn't take risks. I didn't make putts. I was rarely close enough to make putts, actually. The leader shot a 64. 4 strokes are a lot to make up, given the quality of the field.

Day 2: The day went better than yesterday. I tried to be more aggressive even though the conditions were much more challenging. I only got into trouble once, but I made four birdies. I am happy with a 67 but still four behind the leader.

Day 3: They placed me in the final group with the guy I beat in the US Amateur. He is a good player who is very steady. I will have my work cut out for me to catch him. After warmups, Jen took me aside and looked me straight in the face. She said sternly, "You are not someone who coasts to the finish line, Jack. You attack, you compete, and you win. That is who you are. Let's put it all out there. When you see me take my first and pound it into my other palm, we are attacking and competing. "

My sole thought following her pep talk "Yes, Mam. I am not going to disappoint this woman. I love you, Jen, let's Go".

Buoyed by the energy Jen's pep talk provided, I played great. Perhaps some of my best golf ever. I was attacking pins and getting easy birdie putts. I missed a couple but had forgotten that I have one of the best short games in golf. I shot an impressive and tournament-low 61 and won by 3. I realize that when I am in my zone, I don't have to think about shots. I visualize the results, and somehow, my body and the club execute that.

Jen was thrilled. Almost more so than me. Most of my preparation occurs independently. She may feel like more of a spectator than a team member. Today she was a vital team member who kicked me in the butt when I needed it. That made her feel good, I am sure.

Off to Augusta

The win in the Jones Cup kept my number 1 ranking intact. I am approaching this tournament as I do in all the others. Do my thing, put it all out there, and let the cards fall where they may. Tim will be there this time, taking off from his schedule. Fortunately, his professional is not playing in the Masters this year. We are all planning to arrive on Tuesday and to review the course. That will give him some time to prepare and settle in.

We arrived at the clubhouse and were greeted by a concierge who introduced us to some people who coordinated our activities. They are available to us throughout the match if we need them. My first reaction is that I am in total awe of Augusta National. Standing on the clubhouse porch, I reflected on being in this spot a few years prior. Little did I know how fate would bring me here under totally different circumstances. Being here as a participant is very different from being a spectator. I was trying to explain to Jen that it is like the pride you feel when an acquaintance succeeds versus the pride you feel when it is your own family. It's much more personal.

Lee Trevino just walked by. That reminded me of how this place seeps with tradition. Nearly every golfer who aspires to greatness has played here. They had sold on the greatness of this place with all the pictures and memorabilia on the hallways. But then you see all these great former green jacket players mulling about. And then, on the range, you are hitting balls beside the likes of Woods, Nicklaus, Mickelsen, Spieth, and Kupka. The thought of being on the same course with these greats has my head spinning. It was humbling. And that is a gross understatement. Let me put it straight. It was fucking amazing.

Tim and Jen spent a lot of energy trying to keep my emotions in check. They both reminded me repeatedly that I qualified to be here and belonged to compete against the world's best. I am prepared to play my best golf. My game is ready. I am anxious to get after it but nervous as hell.

We invited Glenn to join us. He wanted to come but complained about feeling off, plus he had an important meeting on Friday and his departure would have to wait until that was over. He said he would be watching me from his favorite chair with a Scotch at the ready. I could count on that.

Day 1 - My opening day group comprised Matt Kuchar and Aaron Wise. Matt has won 10 or so tournaments. Aaron Wise was a past rookie of the year. These guys can play.

I had a few minutes before we teed off. I told Matt that he came to my grade school in Atlanta when I was a young kid and told his inspirational story. I respected him for doing that. He joked with me, "You still look like a kid". I responded jokingly, "So do you". Aaron played for the University of Oregon when they won the NCAA national championship. The day they beat Texas was one of the first golf tournaments I remember watching. I felt very much in both player's shadows.

Playing Augusta National was everything I ever expected. It was hard, yet it was beautiful. It wasn't a single thing. The way your ball sat up on the fairway—the incredible greens manicure. The course was so pristine, that it practically willed you to hit great shops. The beautiful old pine trees surround the holes and the old, historic landmarks. It was perfect. To sum it up, the experience was surreal. Strangely, my performance felt almost secondary.

I finished with an immensely satisfying two under par. That was the top amateur performance of the day. Tim and I spoke extensively afterward and agreed that we left a lot out there by playing conservatively. Still, being in the top 10 after day one is pretty damn cool.

Glenn called me right after I finished and congratulated me. He told me that his calendar had cleared and that he would be joining us that evening.

Day 2 - Today, I was teamed up with Shane Lowry from Ireland, and a first-year professional I did not know. Shane has not had much success in the US tour but was more famous in Europe and nearly a legend in Ireland. I remember him from the Ryder Cup. I was asking Tim what he thought the cut line was. He said, "Dude, visualize being on the leaderboard, not around the cut-line." As I thought about it, that was great advice.

During the round, I kept my focus on the present. But the course played much harder. It was hard for me at nearly 7500 yards, but swirling winds added another element. The famous Amen Corner (holes 11-13) ate my lunch today with three bogies.

I watched Jack in an interviewed on the Golf Channel a couple of weeks ago. The question to him was about Augusta, and he spoke about how it can take years to learn the swirling winds. You have to watch certain treetops, he said. A wrong read can distinguish between a shot at the pin or being in the creek.

I finished with an even-par 72. We are still at -2 for the tourney. I made the cut.

Day 3 - Even though I struggled yesterday, I am very much in the hunt at 12th place. I am the only amateur still in the competition. Today, they will team you up with players next to you on the leaderboard, which should be exciting. I will be playing with Scottie Scheffler and Justin Rose. Both are considered among the top players in the world. Scheffler is a long hitter, which gives him a lot of shorter irons to the green. Interestly, he also played in the NCAA tournament I watched with Oregon against Texas. He was paired against Aaron Wise. Rose's game, like mine, relies on control, accuracy and consistency. This will be fun.

The gusty winds from the previous day settled down, and the forecast called for perfect weather. The level of the competition was great for the game. Watching how star players prepare for shots and evaluate their options taught me a lot. Tim's eyes were like saucers as he watched these players perform. Amen Corner was kinder to me today. I played more aggressively today and was rewarded. I picked up two pars and a birdie.

I finished the day with a miraculous 67. This was one of those days where I didn't make all the shots, but I scored incredibly well. Tim reflected on the round and his typically edgy assessment. He said, "Jack, you big turd, you got it done today." I finished with the 4th lowest round of the day and am only three strokes out of the lead.

The tournament is still very much in question. Ten players are within six strokes of the lead. The media seemed highly focused on my position in the tournament, however. They always side with the underdog. No Amateur has ever won the Masters, and only three people have finished 2nd. None of those in the last 70 years. I did a couple of interviews, but Jen helped me keep from getting swallowed up by the media attention. In the player's lounge, it was much the same. Many players were extremely polite, but you could tell that many others were sizing me up. They were probably wondering how this guy does it. Tiger coming over to shake my hand was a real highlight.

Jen was usually very talkative, but she knew my head was exploding with emotions. She knew I would have difficulty sleeping, and it was best to just give me space. Glenn arrived later that evening, and it was good to see him there. I asked him about the mood at the Club. He characterized it as pandemonium. I smiled but he could tell I was fighting back my nerves.

Day 4 I had trouble sleeping and woke up very early with a head full of clutter. I have found solace in spending quiet time looking out over the course as they mowed the grass. I do not tee off until the afternoon, so I thought I could sleep a little before starting my routine. I was playing with Jordan Spieth and Russel Henley. Jordan is, without question, my favorite pro player. He has had a lot of success, but it's more how he conducts himself on the course. He is well-liked and very classy. I am especially drawn to his game, which is much like mine. He is not the longest driver on the tour, although he has added to his length. But he is a killer with his irons and around the greens. His putting is crazy. It will be incredibly awkward meeting him for the first time and thinking of myself as worthy of playing with him.

Before I teed off, Jen came up to me, and I could see the anxiety on her face. She said, "You have risen to every challenge placed in front of me. You got this, and I love you". Shortly after that, Jordan approached me and said, "Hi, I am Jordan Spieth." I responded, "I am Jack Jeffers, and you have been my golf idol since I started playing." Jordan came back and said, laughing, "I guess you haven't followed me long, then. I have been playing since I was a kid. What you have done is incredible.
I am looking forward to playing with you. You have the silkiest swing I think I have ever seen."

My round started exceptionally well, birdieing 3 of the first four holes. I was suddenly atop the leaderboard, tied with Brooks Koepka. I got birdies on 8 or 9 to card a 5-under 31 on the front one ahead of Scheffler. The galleries were enormous. I could not fathom they would be interested in watching me, but there they were. Tim could tell that the pressure on me was real. Tim reminded me that this is just like another round at the Club. We are going to play our game and tune out the noise.

I got through 10-12 with pars. When I thought my prayers were answered at Amen Corner, I lay up conservatively on the legendary par five 13th across the creek. Still, the approach shot had too much backspin and backed into the creek. I could not get up and down and finish with a double bogie 7.

I stayed at ten under until 16. I tried not to watch the leaderboard, but I did notice leaders who were once at 13 under have drifted back to 10. I nearly holed out my tee shot on the par three 16th. I made my putt to push my lead to 1. I got in trouble on 17 off the tee and ultimately had to punch out. I then made the shot of the tournament by hitting a hybrid 230 yards within 3 feet of the flag for a miraculous par. The gallery was electric as I walked up on the 18th green. You dream of walking onto the 18th green with the crowd roaring. I never imagined it could be like this. An already dizzy crowd was sent postal as I pushed my lead to 2 with yet another birdie on 18, dropping a 30-foot putt. The crowd roared for what seemed like 5 minutes as I stretched my lead by 2. OMG was all my mind could process as I walked off the course. Media and fans engulfed me during the stretch up to the official's tent, but fortunately, Tim, Jen, and an official kept things under control amidst the frenzy.

I was in total fog, being the leader in the clubhouse. It is a real advantage, Tim claims. It puts pressure on your competitors to score. They may take risks they might not take otherwise. I'm just glad to be done. I was not ready to see myself as a contender until Jordan approached me and said, "Great round. I think you may make history today." I could hardly talk, my heart was beating so fast. I eked out "there are still a lot of good golfers on the course. Great playing with you today."

Tim was right. The other contenders took chances that hurt them in the end. Leading by 2, when the last group couldn't hole fairway approaches, I knew I had won. As I sat in the players' lounge waiting for the other players to finish, Spieth, Woods, Nicklaus, and a host of other great players came over to offer congratulations.   TV cameras and reporters were in my face seeking interviews. It was coming from every direction. I was not comfortable with that at all. I just wanted the uncertainty to be over so that I could begin to relax.

Finally, I was named the official winner and given notice that the green room ceremony would occur in 10 minutes. I was thinking at that moment, get me out of here so I can breathe. Despite my anxiety, the ceremony was an incredible experience as they pass the torch from Scheffler to me and hand the green jacket to wear. The President of the Masters association spoke of the long, storied history of the tournament, which reminded me of the company of great golfers that I have joined. It was one of those experiences I will never forget.

As the ceremony concluded, Jen approached me urgently while I was still in the afterglow of the ceremony. She muttered something that seemed nonsensical. Realizing I was still in a fog, she grabbed and shook me, informing me we needed to leave immediately. It was Glenn—he had suffered a severe fall and was being rushed to the hospital. Swiftly I paid my final respects and hurried out of the venue. About thirty minutes later, we arrived at the hospital and found Glenn in the emergency unit. Anxiously, we waited in the waiting room, hoping for updates on his condition.

Several hours of anticipation passed before the doctor emerged and delivered the grim diagnosis. "Based on our findings, Glenn experienced a brain aneurysm, leading to loss of consciousness. The fall resulted in significant brain trauma, causing swelling. He is currently in a coma," the doctor explained. "For now, we have stabilized his heart condition. The primary concern is to wait for the swelling to subside and patiently wait for him to emerge from the coma."

Jen grit her teeth and had this look of despair as we hugged. Then Jen started crying. "I hope he will be OK," she said in a whimpering voice. I replied, "Glenn is a tough old bird. He will pull through".

Chapter 13

Glenn faces legal Armageddon

Glenn remained in a coma for nearly three weeks. During that time, the press was abuzz with stories of the amazing performance of Jack Jeffers, the first amateur ever to win the Masters. There were articles across the country about my rise from the Atlanta ghetto to Augusta stardom and features that highlighted nearly every aspect of my life. I could not read this stuff. Glenn, his health, and Jen are the only things that feel important to me right now.

Either Jen or I remained by his side nearly non-stop. Honestly, I was not confident that he would ever wake up. My mind drifted to what I might do or how I might feel without him in my life. We both spent a lot of time in the chapel, asking God to bring him back to us. I had never asked God for anything, but this time was different. Jen reminds me that God answers prayer. Finally, on the morning of the 22nd, he awoke. "Thank you, Jesus!" Jen cried. I thought to myself "Thank you God for bringing him back to us."

One of Glenn's first sights was Jen and I sitting next to him. I'm glad he awoke knowing we were there for him. He routinely downplays his importance in our lives, and I wanted to tell him that we love him, even though it's been tough for me to communicate that. About a day later, they transferred him to Emory Johns Creek Hospital, near the house. The doctors hoped he could come home in about a week.

Jen and I drove over to see Glenn once he arrived at Emory, and he was somewhat lucid. After speaking with him for a few minutes, he was clearly off. The doctors explained it would take him some time to regain mental clarity, but this was different. For example, he did not remember that I played in the Masters. I asked the doctors about what we had observed, and they brought in a specialist to evaluate him.

Their diagnosis revealed that Glenn had experienced what they called retrograde amnesia. They characterized it as a type of amnesia where a person cannot remember events or information before the onset of the amnesia. It is often associated with a brain injury or damage to the brain's hippocampus, which is responsible for the formation and retrieval of memories. They said that in some cases, only the memories from a specific time period are affected. But Glenn's appears to be more extensive and affects memories from several months before the injury.

He remembers Jen. He knows that I am his adopted son, but nearly all his memories from this year seem lost. The specialist said that his memory loss may be temporary or it could be permanent. It's impossible to say.

On top of it all, Glenn is also experiencing motor issues on the left side. He is not able to walk, his left arm is limited, and even his face is affected. His voice is pretty broken and barely discernible. The doctors claim all of this will improve with time and physical therapy. The bottom line is that Glenn will need his family's help and support to regain his life as it used to be.

Yesterday, a reporter stopped me while I was leaving the Hospital. He asked me about my schedule going into preparing for the US Open. Was I planning to participate in any tune-up tournaments? I told him honestly. I said, "With my dad being in the Hospital, thoughts of golf are totally on the back burner. Golf is a game. My family will always be my priority." So the reporter responded, "So, the 'Grand Slam' is definitely out there for you. Are you saying there is a possibility that you won't compete in the US Open?" After a moment of reflection, I said, "Yes," as I got into Glenn's car.

The next day, the paper had a big headline: "Jeffers May Opt out of US Open." .blah, blah, blah. I can hardly read the stuff anymore. Still, I realize I need to make a decision. Jen and I have discussed it. Glenn needs a lot of care. Jen reminds me that we can hire a nurse for him and that she would be willing to help. I reminded her that the tournament was on the West Coast and that it had been a month since I had touched a club.

Still, Jen wants me to compete and can be highly persuasive when she chooses to. I was nearly ready to commit, and then the door rang. It was a guy at the door handing me an envelope. He said, "Glenn has been served."

I opened up the document, and it looks like Glenn is being sued by a company called Angular Realty Holdings for 35 million dollars in economic damages, plus $65 million in non-economic and punitive damages. "Yikes," I exploded, walking around the house pensively as I read. I immediately called up Jen and read the document to her. Once I got beyond the recitals and the rest of the legalese, it said, "...plaintiff alleges Glenn Andrews demonstrated a reckless disregard for the plaintiff and his duties as a legal fiduciary to the plaintiff by canceling a crucial 'deal consummating' meeting, instead opting to attend the Masters Golf tournament where his son was playing. His reckless conduct led to the loss of a critical real estate sale and a substantial business client, not to mention unmeasurable non-financially losses in terms of 'damaged reputation'...."

Jen came over to the house in a near state of hysteria. "What are we going to do, Jack?" speaking almost rhetorically. "I don't know his financial situation, but this will surely bury him," Jen said, sounding pensive as she spoke. Jen then said something important. "I wonder if this guy is somebody trying to cash in on your fame and Glenn's injury?." She then pointed to the plaintiff's name, down at the bottom. She said, "That's Chase Carson from the Club. His name is familiar.." Once I heard the name, I kind of knew what we were up against. I explained to Jen that I had looped a few times for this guy from the Club.

"Let's first visit Glenn to determine what he knows," I said. Jen countered, "Do you think he can process any of this?" "I frankly don't know. I guess we will find out".

We went to the Hospital to see Glenn and show him the suit. We handed this to him, and he read and thumbed through the pages. He seemed to understand but looked puzzled. I asked him if he understood this. He tried to speak but could barely get words out. He shook his head in frustration and pointed to a pen and tablet on the table. He wrote, "I understand the suit, but never heard of Angular ." He then wrote "Call Becca". Becca was his assistant at the law firm. I think he called her a paralegal. I had previously spoken with her to update her on Glenn's status, but I never understood her role, except she seemed to keep things afloat for him when he was gone.

I called her and talked about Glenn's health for a minute or two. I then told her that Angular Realty Holdings is suing Glenn. I told her, "Glenn does not seem to remember who they are. Do you know?" Becca then replied. "Boy, that's not good," understanding that Glenn has experienced memory loss. "Angular is a big and active client, she said. "Glenn formed a partnership and drafted various sales agreements for this big land sale involving the Hospital. I had heard from a local news report that the Hospital decided to go a different direction." As I described the suit to her, her reaction was, "OMG. How can Glenn defend himself if he can't remember." I told her I was thinking the very same thing. I added that Glenn seems generally clear-minded, although he can barely speak. I told her that I would try to act as the go-between. I then asked if she could prepare a file on Angular for Glenn to review. She said she would drop it by.

I went to Glenn and asked him if there was anyone else I should contact. He wrote, "My brother Mel." Given how hard it was to track him down, I gathered that he and Glenn were not particularly close. I asked Becca about him, and she said he is the older brother who was also a lawyer at the firm but has since retired. She mentioned that they had a family quarrel a while back and sensed there was ongoing tension.

After we brought Glenn home, Mel came over and greeted me casually. He congratulated me on the Masters and then proceeded to converse with Glenn. I could not hear much from their conversation, but I did catch Mel saying, "This is what happens when you take on risky clients ', sounding like someone highly irritated. Becca came by and dropped off the Angular file. She paid her respects to Glenn, but I saw she was noticeably cool toward Mel as she left.

After Mel left, Glenn sat in his chair and reviewed the file. Jen and I cooked up some pasta while Glenn read and sipped on his Scotch. He usually held his Scotch with his left hand, but this time, he held it with his right. It was apparent it was not strong enough to hold the glass. He then wrote something down. "I am probably not supposed to be drinking. Fuck them!" with a subtle crooked smile. After dinner, I sat at the table with Glenn and discussed the case.

"Are we in trouble here?" I asked. "Yes," Glenn said, struggling to get the word out. On his tablet, he wrote, "..if I can't remember. I then asked him if Mel was going to help me. His response was sad. He said, "Maybe. Don't count on it."

.

After we got Glenn to bed, I reread the suit and reviewed the file in detail as Jen read. I didn't understand a lot of what I read, but at the same time, I was fascinated by the legal principles at work in this case and how they are used to prove one side or the other.

I waited until Jen reached a stopping point so I could grab her attention. I then went over and sat next to her. "You know what?" I said. "There is no way I can play golf while Glenn is embroiled in this. This case will ruin Glenn forever, and it appears Mel can't–or won't–step up to help him. I hope you understand, but Glenn really, really needs me."

"I am trying to understand. I know you are a smart guy, but remember, you're not a lawyer. We can hire the best legal minds. We can hire the best caretakers. Shouldn't you be doing what you do best?" I countered. "Yes, I get it. I honestly don't know how I can help him yet. I just know deep in my core that I can." I paused and walked around, trying to hide the tears rolling down my eyes. "Jen, I owe Glenn everything…that is a debt I've always wondered how I would ever repay. Maybe this is a way of making a downpayment on that debt."

Jen then came over to me to wipe my tears. She said, "You probably thought I fell in love with you because you were a great golfer. No. I fell in love with you because you are a wonderful human being and a man of principle. I do understand and love you for it." she said as she held my face. She then said, "I know you will rise to the occasion. You always do. Play this hole like it is the toughest par five you have ever played and Glenn will be fine. ".

Jen fell asleep on the couch and woke up around 3 am with me sitting beside her. I had my nose in a pile of books. Jen asked me with a hazy, sleepy voice, "What are you reading?" I told her I found a few books in Glenn's library. I held up the books as I explained them to her. One was "Essentials of Business Law" by Jeffrey F. Beatty. Another was ""The Law of Professional Responsibility" by Ronald D. Rotunda". The other was "The Art of Advocacy: Briefs, Motions, and Writing Strategies of America's Best Lawyers" by Noah Messing. I told her I was finding some really helpful information here. She said she was going to bed. I told her I would stay up and read for a while.

Jen woke up to the smell of coffee brewing. She came down the stairs rubbing her eyes. Glenn was sitting in his chair eating breakfast, and I was writing on an easel I found in the attic. There was a pile of books and loose papers all around. Jen could tell I was very much into what I was doing. Certainly, it's too much to stop and chat. Jen grabs a piece of toast and tells me she needs to get to the office but will see me this evening. I went back to my research.

Jen returned to the house twelve hours later with me in essentially the same place she found me, with my nose in a book. Realizing I had been glued to this for a while, I put my books down and then asked her about her day. She said her office manager gave her notice today. The office manager suggested she was a victim of some inappropriate advances that created a hostile workplace. Jen said, "I asked her why she didn't come see me. She shrugged her shoulders and then left. I won't be surprised if that ends up being a lawsuit." I responded to Jen, saying, "I read somewhere that if you think a suit is coming, get ahead of it and prepare. Ask Glenn what you might do. "Great idea. I will," Jen said.

Jen then said, "Tell me about your easel. "I found this in the attic," I said. This book on case planning suggests that it is a good idea to diagram all the facts you know so that you can continually study and refer to them. Glenn already told me he doesn't remember anything but has been communicating background information throughout the day.

"Here is what we know," I said

1) March 28 - Parties have a conference call to discuss the Angular proposal (s=GNotes)

2) March 30, 3 pm - Hospital calls Angular - Verbally accepts offer. (s=Complaint)

3) March 30, 5 pm - CC [Chase Carson] calls Glenn to draft papers (s=GNotes)

4) April 3, 1 pm - Glenn calls the Hospital legal team - he forwards 1st draft (s=GNotes)

5) April 4, 10 am - The Hospital Legal team calls Glenn to schedule a signing meeting for 4/7 at 10 am (s=GNotes)

6) April 6, 2:15 pm- Glenn calls Jack' My schedule is now free,' be there tonight (s=Jack)

7) April 6, 2:30 - CC discovers the meeting has been canceled unilaterally (s=Complaint)

8) April 6, 6 pm - CC calls Glenn to restart completion of agreement (s=Complaint)

9) April 7, 1 pm - Glenn calls the Hospital and discovers they found a new property (s=Complaint)

10) April 10 - 9 am Hospital legal team tells CC their deal off (s=Complaint)

   s=Source

As I was talking to Jen, I started running things past her. "We know Glenn is very precise and deliberate in what he does. He is not a flake. He doesn't blow off meetings or get confused. I cannot believe Glenn would make an error on something so important." Jen then counters, trying to give me something to consider, "Is it possible Jack wanted to go to Augusta so bad that he made a mistake subconsciously?". "I had considered that for a moment," I explained. "except Glenn wasn't originally planning to go to the tourney until the weekend. He knew he needed to finish this transaction before leaving for Augusta. He wasn't trying to skate out. There is obviously something here that we are missing".

Over the next two weeks, I spent most of my time researching and working on the case with laser focus. I have already finished the Spring Term finals. I notified the US Open people that I would not participate, citing personal reasons. I have been studying everything I can get my hands on that is remotely relevant to this case.

Mel tells me that Glenn is scheduled to be deposed next week. I asked him if we had scheduled a deposition with Chase Carson. He said, "No". I then asked if we needed to hire another attorney. He said, "No". My first observation is that he is about as talkative as Glenn. My 2nd observation is that he is less-than-engaged. I don't know why that would be. Glenn will be ruined if he loses. I sense he does not care, and I do not understand why. Despite all this drama, I am committed and will not let Glenn lose.

I already had voiced concerns about Glenn giving his deposition to a room full of people. I requested Mel postpone the deposition until Glenn improves healthwise, citing health concerns still affecting memory and speech. The Judge rejected that suggestion. What he did agree to were written questions.

Chase Carson is the critical character from our perspective. We need to get specific information from him. The best way to approach this is to think about what information you need and construct questions that might lead you to that answer. An advantage of face-to-face depositions is that you can pursue a line of questions and improvise as you go. I requested Mel set up a deposition for Chase Carson. Jen suggests that it seems funny that I am initiating the activities, not Mel. I told her, I agree.

Jen had her own strategy in the works. She had been reading that people with amnesia can regain lost memories using certain visual and auditory stimuli. She called these triggers. Jen played replays of the Masters on TV. She found a picture of Chase Carson on Facebook—various pictures of his office, the Club, Jack, and I. So far, no luck.

Team Andrews adamantly agrees that Glenn would never have been irresponsible or self-serving in an important business matter. Our ultimate solution is for Glenn's memory to return. The odds of that happening improve as we extend the process. Barring that, we need to figure out what really happened. That is my mission.

This weekend is the US Open. I told Jen that it would be too hard to watch. I have already been in contact with the Golf Channel, who wanted to do a story on me. I declined. Jen thinks I should make a public appearance. I told her I would consider it.

Our wedding plans have also been affected, and I believe Jen is considering the impact. Initially, we had hoped to have our ceremony in Scotland during The Open Championship. However, I'm beginning to think that the trip and my participation in the tournament may not be feasible, given Glenn's current condition. While Glenn shows signs of improvement, such as increased mobility in his left hand and the ability to speak, progress has been slow. He is also regaining some mental acuity, but there still seems to be a lot of confusion. To aid in his recovery, we are taking him to the rehabilitation center three times a week, and they appear to be satisfied with his progress. However, based on the pace of his rehabilitation, it could take months, if not longer, to fully recover.

I need to make a tough decision about Scotland soon. Based on the current state, the conversation with Jen will not be easy.

Mel has scheduled a deposition of Chase Carson in a couple of weeks. Operating in the background, I have been working on drafting questions. Our entire focus has to center on a single day. April 6th. Precisely what happened between 10 am and 2 pm. From looking at Glenn's phone records that I recovered, Glenn received a phone call from Carson at 1:50, 25 minutes before he called me. What happened during that call?

    6a - April 6 - 1:50 am Carson calls Jack (s=GA Phone records)

    6b - April 6 - 2:00 am Jack calls Hospital Legal (s=GA Phone records)

6c - April 6, 2:15 pm- Glenn calls Jack' My schedule is now free,' coming tonight (s=Jack)

Assuming we trust that Glenn acted responsibly and in his client's best interests, that suggests his conversation must have directed Glenn to terminate or push back the closing of the transaction. I already called the Hospital Legal team to ask about their discussion with Glenn, but they have refused to talk to me since I am not an affiliate with Andrews Law.

In response, I have directed Mel to subpoena the Hospital Legal team to provide a written description of the phone conversation.

I have also requested Mel to subpoena Carson's phone records for April 6th. He did, and a phone record arrived a week later. I instantly noticed that the record was heavily redacted and was a photocopy, not an unredacted original, as we requested. Mel made another request for the phone record. Originals only. They did not comply.

Carson's deposition is scheduled in about a week. However, due to what we argued was his failure to comply, we successfully pushed back the depositions for a month. During that time, Glenn's memory may return. We can only hope.

With July approaching, I finally spoke earnestly about our plans for July. I told Jen that I have a greater purpose in front of me than golf. Jen reluctantly understood, showing a lot of disappointment. "Are you sure?" she cried. I nodded yes. She hoped to see me in The Open Championship, which she knew in her heart would not be plausible. I have not played since the Masters, and she knew I would not be ready. I promised her we would schedule a trip to Scotland to marry as soon as Glenn was better.

Mel came over to the house, and he reviewed our case with Glenn. I could tell I had not garnered much respect in his eyes, but at least he included me in his discussions. Mel made another attempt to delay Carson's deposition. The Judge unfortunately denied the request.

Mel and I conducted the deposition at Glenn's office. Mel and I were hosting it, along with a court reporter. Glenn and Jen were there also, although he and Jen did not speak. Mel had not prepared any questions, and he was figuring I would. Fortunately, I was ready. There was much more protocol than I understood from my readings. Mel started with what seemed like boilerplate questions: "For the record, please state your name..." After a set of introductory questions for Mr. Carson, it became my turn to 'interrogate.

"Mr Carson, tell us what you were doing on April 6th between 10 am and 2 pm". Carson responded, "I enjoyed breakfast at the Club and watched the Masters."

"Mr Carson. Did you make any phone calls during that time? "I asked. Mr Carson: "I took a call from my wife. Then I called Mr Andrews [Glenn] to determine the legal preparation and closing status?"

"What did he say?" I asked. Caron responds, "Mr Andrews said he had nothing new to report." I asked, "Is it your position, Mr Carson, that Mr Andrews intentionally pushed back on the closing so that he could attend the Masters?". Carson replied, "Yes, although I suppose he could have simply forgotten about it." "Were you aware, Mr. Carson, that Mr. Andrews called the Hospital Legal team after your phone call? Any thoughts on what that call might have been about? "I asked. Mr. Carson responded, "No idea."

"That concludes my questions," I said.

After the room cleared of the plaintiff team, Jen said she noticed something she wanted to share with me. She said, "Did you notice that when Carson said 'No idea,' he looked down? I have read that it is usually a sign of dishonesty. "I responded, "I think you are right. He is as dirty as hell. We just need to prove it."

A couple of days later, I was reviewing my email. In today's inbox was an email from the USGA informing me that this year's US Amateur was open to anyone with a handicap under 2.4 or lower. That got me thinking about golf handicaps, a system measuring golfers' ability. Handicaps provide a system allowing average golfers to compete fairly against even the best golfers. It is all based on scores of actual rounds.

As I reflected, I remembered that Mr Carson was very preoccupied with proper handicap collection, which means every qualifying score must be posted and used to compute a fair handicap. I wonder if he played golf on April 6th. I searched the USGA website where handicaps and posted scores are maintained and…. I shouted out, "Hey Jen, come here quick." A moment later, she walked in, and I said, "Check this out. Carson played golf on Thursday. He lied". Jen then says something obvious, yet pertinent. "Why?". "Well, we are going to find out why. "I said.

I immediately hopped in the Jeep and headed out to the Club. I went to the pro and asked if he had any record of Carson playing golf on Thursday, April 6th. The dispute was very well known around the Club, and the pro shop employees were instructed to avoid taking sides. Glenn was correct and suggested that would be the case. The pro shop employee said, "They did not show any record of him playing." I then went to the loop shed, where there were a couple of loopers. I sat around the table and chatted for a while. None of them remembered looping for Carson that day. Because he is a big tipper, his loops are well-remembered. I was walking back onto the course, and one of the loopers said to me, "Hey Jack, I don't know if this would be helpful, but Riley Koontz, who lives on the number 3 tee box, has been giving out bloody marys to golfers going by. Maybe he knows something. "Thanks," and immediately grabbed a cart and drove up to number 3.

I approached the tee box and saw Carl Kootz and his wife sitting on their porch watching the golfers. I approached them, and they said, "Jack, what a pleasure." I sat down and chatted with him for a few moments. He had a thousand questions about how it felt to be Masters champion, wear the Green jacket, and play with all those famous names. "He also asked, "How is Glenn doing? "Apparently, they were good friends at the Club. I spent at least 10 minutes talking when I turned the conversation around. I asked them if they watched me at the Masters. Carl said, "All four days." "Were you also out here?" Sure. We were going back and forth. I asked, "On Thursday, do you remember if Chase Carson came through?" "It's funny that you would ask. We invited him over for a drink. You were on the TV, and he seemed totally disinterested when we pointed you out. He then took a phone call." "Did you catch any of that?" I asked. Carl said, "Not really, but I did hear him mention something about getting more money." He then called someone right back, "and I heard something again "...holding out for more money. That's all I know." Chase then took off and played his round.

I called Mel, telling him what I had learned, and he said to make sure they would agree to sign an affidavit of what they told you. I approached Carl, and he agreed. "Anything to help Glenn," he said. Fortunately, it was apparent that Chase Carson was not among his favorites.

We secured the affidavit from Carl that proved Carson was lying in his deposed testimony. At about the same time, we received the written responses from the Hospital legal team that indicated Glenn's call on April 6th asked to push back the meeting until Monday. We had asked them to comment on anything that might have contributed to the closure of their negotiations with Angular. They refused to answer. Here is now what we know.

     6a - April 6 - 1:50 am Carson calls Jack (s=GA Phone records)

     6b - April 6 - 1:55 am CC receives a call from someone and discuss getting more money (s=Koontz affidavit)

     6c - April 6 - 2:00 am Jack calls Hospital Legal asking for push-back to Monday (s=GA Phone records)

     6d - April 6, 2:15 pm- Glenn calls Jack' My schedule is now free,' coming tonight (s=Jack)

By looking at the facts, it was evident that Carson called Glenn to push back on the closing to see if he could extract more money from the deal. That explains why he will not provide the original, unredacted phone records.

That evening, Mel and Glenn strategized and agreed it would be a good time to move for what they called a "summary judgment ." In that motion, we ask the Judge to rule in our favor, given the evidence submitted. If he agrees, the case is over. Our case is based upon a preponderance of evidence, and the plaintiff filed fraudulent testimony.

Today, Mel and I drafted our motion. It included the fraudulent deposition testimony and the written responses from the Hospital's legal team. We also had the Koontz affidavit and my affidavit stating that Glenn's call after his conversation with Carson indicated his schedule was now free. Andrews thought he was instructed to push the meeting back to Monday. The Judge rejected our motion but did issue a stern warning suggesting he would reconsider our request if Carson did not produce the original, unredacted phone records as requested.

Angular knew that the unredacted phone records would lead us to their source of the guise, which we later learned consisted of an internal plant feeding information to Angular. Their plant told Carson they could up their take by $10 million if they waited. Apparently, this plant was discovered and fired, and the Hospital moved to a different property.

We received a letter a few days later stating they were withdrawing their lawsuit. Jen and I, Glenn, were sitting on the edge of our chairs, anticipating the letter's arrival. We finally received a call from Glenn's law office and literally sprang out of our chairs. What a great win for our family.

Usually, when I competed in a tournament, there was little on the line beyond my goals and perhaps my ego. In this case, the tournament's outcome was either a return to normal life or a total collapse for Glenn. I have been grappling with those two paradigms for a while now. I love golf–don't get me wrong here–but golf is just a game. Sure, watching golf fills up a lot of empty lives. But those will be filled in other ways even if Jack Jeffers is not playing on their TV screen. I need something more meaningful in my life than golf.

I feel like a career in law might be a way to make my life more meaningful.

Chapter 14

An Astonishing Discovery

With Glenn's legal issues behind us and Glenn seemingly on the mend, it will allow Jen and I to spend more time as a couple.

It has been about 4 months since Glenn came out of his coma. His mobility is slowly returning. He can speak better. He can walk a little with a cane. He even swore at me a little. It seems every day brings him a little closer to normalcy.

As a complete surprise, Glenn's memory just returned. One day, he was sitting in his chair watching the news, and it was like he had just awoken from a deep sleep. He yelled, "Jack. You won the Masters!" in a slurred, unusually confident voice. He sat down with us and recited all the previously forgotten things. It was great to have him back. I am even more glad that he will eventually recapture his life.

With Glenn's memory returned, we confirmed that Carson instructed Glenn to push back the signing, hoping to escalate the price. That move obviously backfired on him. Jen taught me a new word I had heard but did not understand. Karma. It is nature's way of evening the score between good and bad guys.

Glen appeared before the Club membership committee and requested Chase Carson's removal due to ethics violations. Glenn spoke to them about a lawsuit filed to exploit Glenn's amnesia. It was a case based on falsehoods. The committee found Glenn's arguments compelling and agreed that Carson violated their ethics policy egregiously. What made matters worse was that those violations were against a fellow member. They voted unanimously to revoke Carson's membership. I would have loved being a fly on the wall when Carson received the news.

I just enrolled at the Emory University Law School in Southeast Atlanta. I received special dispensation due to my family's longstanding legacy. I plan to clerk for Glenn while I'm in school, and he is still in rehab. Once I complete school and pass the Bar exam, I will join Andrews Law and work side-by-side as Glenn's partner for as long as he wants to practice. I have said many times there is no way I could ever repay Glenn for everything he had done for me. Being like the son he lost, helping him rebuild his life and career, and being a part of his legacy feels like the right thing for me to do.
Jen and I talked about this extensively and, at times, contentiously. In her heart, Jen felt my golf game was a special blessing from God. "To turn my back on God's gift is to discredit it," she argued. I explained that I recognized the gift golf gave me. Also, I was not planning to turn my back on golf, but I don't see it as the centerpiece of my life. I told her I have not ruled out playing in next year's Masters. After all, I am the defending champion and have a lifetime exemption. I want to stay open-minded about being an active, competitive golfer in the future.

Jen has reduced her day-to-day role at the spirits distributorship to primarily part-time. She plans to maintain her position on the board, allowing her to retain control of the business. It also keeps her active in the more significant issues but will give her enough freedom to pursue other interests.

Jen spends most of her free time working at the Jack Jeffers Foundation. The size of the Foundation has grown significantly after the Master's win. It currently claims assets in excess of 1 million dollars. New contributions arrive daily.

Cole was the Foundation's first benefactor. After hitting the rock button, he finally agreed to accept help. Thanks in large part to Jen's urging, I finally disclosed to him that I was his son and needed him in my life. He started crying. Glenn was right that it seemed to provide a critical purpose during rehab. The Foundation put him through the detox and rehabilitation program and got him set up to attend support meetings. After he left, I got him a paid internship as a training instructor at the Club. He will work closely with Jeff, bringing him along slowly as he proves himself. I made it clear there is zero tolerance for any drug-related backstep. He has a world of support if he experiences a weak moment. He can become increasingly involved in our family as he proves himself. That will start with attending Sunday church and then Sunday dinner.

Jen's biggest issue currently is getting ready for the wedding. We have set a date of October 21. Elspeth graciously offered to host our wedding at her place. I did not realize then that she owned a castle in Carnoustie. It is large enough that she has graciously agreed to accommodate all attendees. Given the location, our wedding should be unique even though the ceremony will involve a small number of attendees.

Word from Elspeth

Jen and Elspeth would Facetime frequently, almost daily. There was a lot of coordination in lining up the priest, the flowers, food, etc. While Scotland is part of the British Empire, even though English is the primary language, there are still many cultural anomalies that Elspeth understands, especially when dealing with locals. Jen thought she could take that on, but after many rounds of frustration, she realized she needed someone on the ground to coordinate.

Interspersed during her coordination activities, Elspeth decided after many years to go to her mum Roslin's cottage. Elspeth and Roslin lived together in Selkirk until she left in 1966. After Roslin retired as a city worker, she moved to the country and lived in this cabin until she died in 1995.

This morning, Elspeth called Jen while she was at work. Unfortunately, Jen could not take the call. Elspeth didn't really want to talk about the wedding this time anyway. She had an exuberance to her voice that was divergent from the usually dignified, classy Elspeth we were used to. This time, she could not wait for Jen and decided to leave a lengthy video message.

Start of Video Message
"This is a braw day, Jen and Jack

I have been pawing through Roslin's cabin. After you were here, I realized how little I knew about her. I was hoping to find things there that could tell her story and connect me with my past. After a few days of looking at her business documents and financial records, I had not learned much except that Roslin was not wealthy. I then made my way to the attic. I found a few heirlooms, a broken antique clock from the 1700's, and some memorabilia there. The most significant find, however, was a box with some letters and a journal. It was very revealing. I will box these up so that you can have them.

Here is what I learned. Roslin grew up in Edinburgh. Her dad was a golfer who worked as an instructor at a local golf course. He was outstanding and played in The Open Championship in 1930. One of Roslin's favorite memories was being the caddie for her dad as a teenager when he was paired up with Bobby Jones. She continued working as a caddie and female instructor around St Andrews. She described it as a great experience where she met a lot of famous golfers like Bobby Jones, Sam Sneed, Walter Hagen, and Byron Nelson. She said her relationship with these golfers was polite. However, there was always an undercurrent of suggestiveness that made her uncomfortable. There are some pictures of Roslin. She was a bonnie lass indeed and probably very popular among the gents.

Roslin met Gramme in 1935 back in Selkirk. She describes her romantic relationship with him as a whirlwind. He was very handsome and swept her off her feet. They were married in 1938, just before he left for war.

In Glasgow during WWII, her parents were killed during a German air raid. It wasn't that long afterward that Gramme, who was a member of the RAF [Royal Air Force] as a fighter pilot, was killed in action. He died in 1942 in an air raid over Belgium. Roslin was devastated and depressed. She loved him very much. There was an entry for Tobias Laird, a cousin of sorts. He was in the Royal Army and visited Roslin once to offer 'comfort' to a grieving widow if ye git my drift. From what I can gather, that visit was not welcome.

There is a several-year gap in her history. But here's where it gets interesting", speaking with Scottish slang.

"There was a letter from Bobby Jones dated January 12, 1946. He said he would attend the British Amateur golf event at St. Andrews in the first week of June and would love to see her. Roslin agreed.

Roslin was not one to 'kiss and tell,' but in a journal entry after that meeting, she indicated the time she spent with Bobby along the coast was the most beautiful three days of her life. 'Bobby was the most loving, affectionate, and caring man she ever met, wrote Roslin. I did some math and realized I was born approximately nine months later.
This was one of the last entries in her journal. Not long after, she moved to Selkirk and bore me. There were a couple more letters from Bobby, but there was no indication that she answered them or ever went to see him again. She wanted to keep her pregnancy and the bairn [child] a secret.

If all of this is true, that makes me the daughter of the legendary Bobby Jones. Jack would be his great-grandson.

How's that for a bit of news for a Thursday? Safe journeys to ye. Bye
End of Video Message

Jen was with Glenn when I arrived back home from school. When I entered the door, Jen instantly grabbed me and said, "You gotta sit down and watch this.

We watched, and I just sat there in amazement when the video was over. Glenn, who was half listening but saw our faces in full view, wondered what all the fuss was about. Jen replied, "Jack just found out he is very likely the great-grandson of Bobby Jones."
Glenn then says something profound, speaking in his somewhat gravelly voice, "Damn!" then with a pause. "That kind of explains a lot, doesn't it?".

Jen nodded and smiled, realizing Elspeth's findings connected so many dots.
I was still shaken from the explosive finding but became more at ease after some thought.

In an uncanny and almost serendipitous manner, Bobby Jones and my life share an eerie resemblance. From my research, it became apparent that golf came effortlessly to Bobby. His style of play bore striking similarities to mine—steady and accurate, with an unyielding composure even in the face of immense pressure. As exceptional as he was on the greens, Bobby refused to let competitive golf define him entirely. Even though he cherished the game, golf was not the only passion in his life. Like me, Bobby was always wary of the all-consuming nature of competitive golf and realized that was something he needed to constrain.

In another bit of uncanny luck, Bobby possessed a natural aptitude for mathematics and sciences, finding joy in constructing things. It was only fitting that he found solace in engineering, exploring his logical side. However, what truly is astounding is his journey into the legal realm. Following his parents' footsteps, Bobby emerged as a renowned and respected lawyer, a testament to his multifaceted abilities. Beyond these remarkable accomplishments, he pursued diverse interests, even venturing into golf course design.

As I reflect upon the parallels between our lives, I must also recognize where our paths diverged. Bobby always played the game from the fairway. He was the son of an aristocrat and grew up in highly privileged surroundings. Conversely, my life was played from the rough using the 'golf is the game of life' metaphor. My life was not lived on Easystreet but from a backroom alley. Thankfully, Glenn showed me a life I could never have imagined six years earlier. He also taught me values and the importance of helping others.

Glenn once told me, "The first step to becoming wealthy is to understand what is valuable." At the time, I assumed having a big bank account, cars, money, and fame defined wealth. However, in his quiet wisdom, Glenn knew things such as family, faith, friends, character and integrity were even more valuable and honored. Bobby Jones knew this also and lived his life accordingly.

I also will have to accept that I must live my life in the shadow of maybe the greatest golfer to ever play the game. For that, I should not complain, for within that shadow lies the presence of an extraordinary man who left an indelible mark on the world.

Made in the USA
Columbia, SC
26 October 2024

5ee38934-9030-41c8-bd21-90e4b52bbad4R01